"Breathe life into its original meaning,
while breathing out the fumes
of distortion."

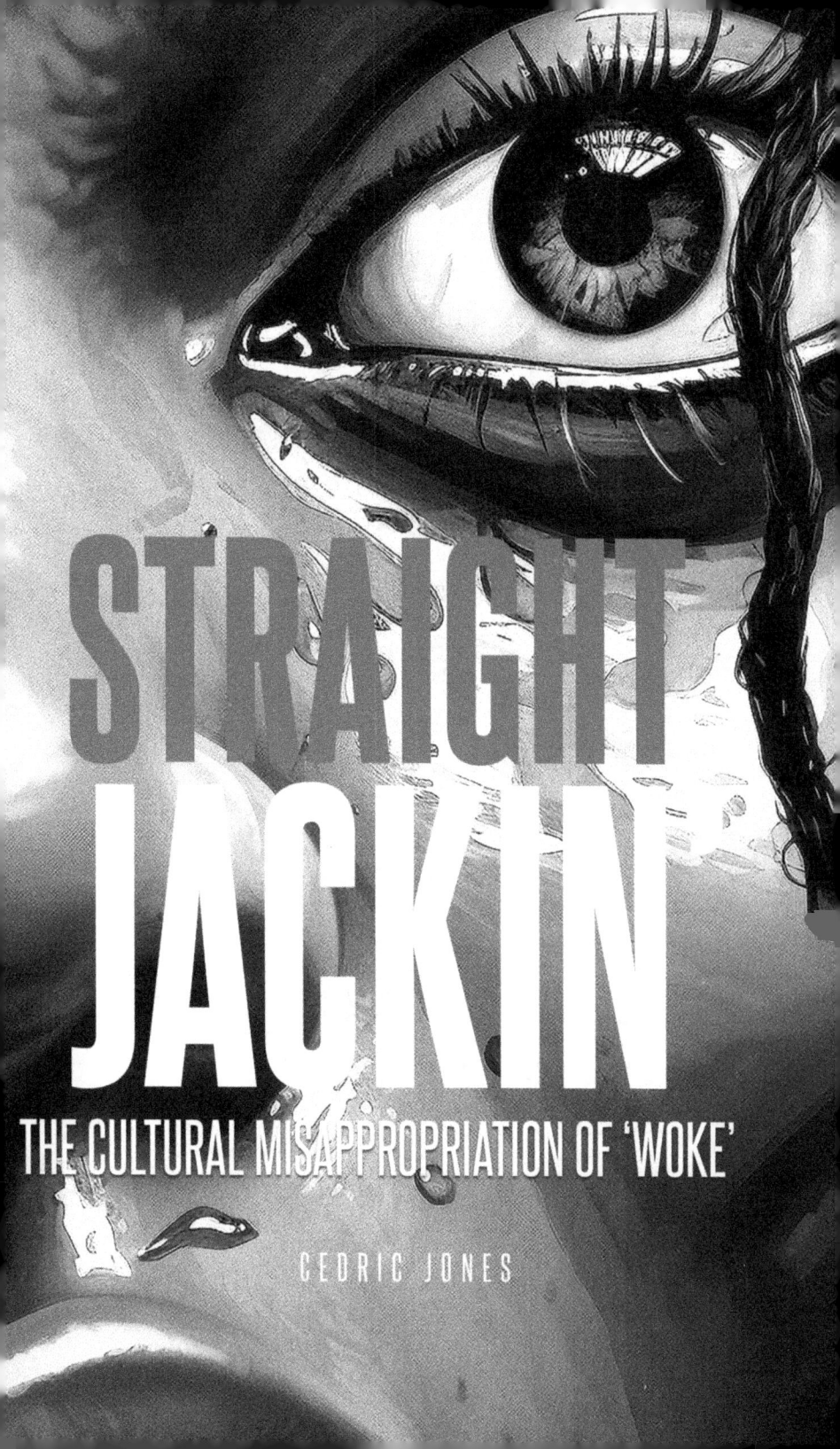

# STRAIGHT JACKIN

## THE CULTURAL MISAPPROPRIATION OF 'WOKE'

CEDRIC JONES

ISBN 978-0-9763065-2-8 (paperback)

Book Cover and Inside Art by Cyphur + Art & Design

This book is dedicated to you, my fierce and compassionate warriors, who have shown me the true meaning of resilience and strength. As we journey through these pages together, let it serve as a reminder to always keep the flame of "woke" burning bright within your hearts. In a world that constantly seeks to challenge and redefine its ideals, I am inspired by your unwavering determination to stand up for what is just and right. May you continue to fearlessly champion the causes that matter, to be the voices of change, and to never shy away from advocating for a more inclusive and compassionate society. Your spirit and tenacity give hope to a better tomorrow. I am immensely proud to be your dad and to witness the positive impact you both make in the world.

# INSIDE...

# WHY THIS BOOK IS NECESSARY

Before you read this, please understand that this is an academic exercise. The journey into the depths of Straight Jackin' begins with a critical imperative—an understanding of the profound implications surrounding the appropriation of my culture's vernacular. This book will read more like academic text than spine tingling thriller, but let's be clear, our culture has had so many things stolen from us, education on the matter is completely justifiable. I was compelled by disgust to author this text, without my usual opines, and was reminded of an Ice Cube song penned while he recorded with the likes of Hank Shocklee and Public Enemy, "Jackin' For Beats". In this case, the focal point of our exploration is the term "woke" in all of its misinterpreted splendor.

This literary endeavor aspires to construct a foundational groundwork, one that paves the way for the uninformed and extends an olive branch to the far-right conservative fringe. We are embarking on a profound quest to untangle the complex web woven by those who have appropriated the cultures of others, even within our very own. And yes, we confront the audacious belief held by some that they can truly grasp the essence of our vernacular, dismissing the rich reservoir of language-crafting skills we possess.

Through these pages, the narrative reveals itself as an intricate tapestry, interwoven with themes of cultural preservation and identity. It is an invitation to unlearn and relearn, a process of introspection and self-awareness that empowers us to embrace authenticity in our advocacy. The power of empathy and attentive listening emerges as essential pillars, forging connections that bridge the divides of diverse worldviews.

Let us not underestimate the strength derived from acknowledging our own imperfections and cultivating humility in our journey. For in doing so, we nurture an atmosphere of collective resilience and empowerment.

As we traverse this literary landscape, we find ourselves grappling with ethical considerations that demand our unwavering dedication to justice and inclusivity. At its core, this is a call to action, a summons to elevate the voices of the marginalized and honor their narratives. Their experiences become the harmonious symphony that enriches our cultural mosaic.

Yet, amidst the pursuit of progress, we are not immune to criticism and resistance. Challenges emerge, but it is through these trials that we forge the strength to navigate the complex path ahead.

So, my cherished companion in this transformative journey, let us celebrate the authenticity of our diverse cultural expressions. Let us seize this opportunity to empower ourselves and others with the profound wisdom that lies within these pages.

This path toward a genuine awakening extends beyond the confines of a single individual. It embraces the interconnectivity of our stories and struggles, embracing the intersectionality that breathes life into our collective existence. As we partake in this exchange of knowledge, we foster a shared vision of a more just and compassionate world, embracing the power of our cultural diversity.

By reading this book you have now become a bearer of this torch. I extend my deepest gratitude for the privilege of embarking on this literary journey together. May the wisdom and insights gleaned from Straight Jackin' continue to ignite the flames of awareness, as we embark on our individual and communal quests to nurture a society that celebrates cultural appreciation and understanding.

Until we meet again on the horizon of enlightenment, let this knowledge be the catalyst that propels us toward transformative change. In unity, we shall advance, unyielding in our pursuit of a brighter and more equitable future.

# STRAIGHT JACKIN

## THE CULTURAL MISAPPROPRIATION OF 'WOKE'

CEDRIC JONES

*"In this world, where there is a blatant misuse of the word 'woke,'
true enlightenment has become a rare and precious jewel."*

# THE PRIMER

## The Enigma of "Woke"

Within the intricate fabric of language, certain words take on an enigmatic quality, encapsulating multilayered meanings, cultural significance, and rich historical context. "Woke" is one such term, a word that has transcended its humble origins in African American Vernacular English (AAVE) to become a rallying cry for social consciousness and justice. Yet, despite its prominence in contemporary discourse, the true essence of "woke" remains elusive, obscured by the myriad interpretations and co-optations it has undergone.

Derived from the AAVE expression "stay woke," the term "woke" originally denoted an awakening to social and political realities. It called upon individuals to remain vigilant, cognizant of the pervasive injustices and systemic racism that plagued society. It represented an empowered state of heightened awareness, a commitment to challenge the status quo, and an unwavering dedication to advocating for a more just and equitable world.

To comprehend the true significance of "woke," we must embark on a journey through history, tracing its roots to the civil rights and Black liberation movements of the 20th century. It was in these crucibles of activism that the term first gained traction, resonating with those who fought tirelessly for racial equality. During this time, "woke" was imbued with profound urgency, signifying the awakening of collective consciousness and the imperative to dismantle oppressive systems.

However, like a river meandering through diverse landscapes, the term "woke" did not remain confined to its original context. Instead, it flowed into broader waters, embracing a myriad of social and political causes, each contributing to the river's ever-evolving current of meaning.

"Woke" took on a deeper meaning. It became more than just a word; it became a philosophy, an ethos that animated the pursuit of social justice. Within the civil rights and Black liberation movements, being "woke" represented an awakened consciousness, one that transcended mere awareness to catalyze action. To be "woke" was not passive; it was an active commitment to challenge injustice, to confront discrimination, and to pave the way for a brighter future.

As we navigate the intricate terrain of "wokeness," we must tread carefully, mindful of the historical legacy that shaped the term's original significance. It is a term that has journeyed through time, evolving, expanding, and at times, becoming entangled in unforeseen webs of interpretation and manipulation. To fully grasp the complexities of "woke," we must embark on a voyage of exploration, seeking to unravel its enigmatic layers, honor its historical roots, and discern its relevance in the present-day landscape of social justice and activism.

## The Transformation and Expansion of "Woke"

Language is a living entity, subject to the currents of cultural change and societal shifts. As "woke" emerged from its historical cocoon, it underwent a metamorphosis, transforming from a specific call to action within the civil rights and Black liberation movements to a more broadly encompassing symbol of social and political awakening. Its wings expanded to carry its essence across diverse movements, embracing causes beyond racial equality.

In the wake of the civil rights era, "woke" gradually shed its narrow definition to accommodate a more inclusive understanding. It became an umbrella term for various forms of social consciousness, capturing the ethos of activism that sought to challenge systems of oppression. From feminism to environmentalism, "woke" embraced a growing array of social justice movements, infusing each with its original spirit of heightened awareness and advocacy.

As the world witnessed the rise of globalization and interconnectedness, "woke" transcended geographical boundaries. Its allure crossed cultures, transcending linguistic barriers to resonate with communities worldwide. Whether in the fight for LGBTQ+ rights or the battle against economic inequality, being "woke" came to symbolize an acute awareness of injustice and the resolve to combat it, irrespective of the cause.

The transformation of "woke" into a global phenomenon sparked a collective awakening, heralding a new era of societal consciousness. The proliferation of social media platforms further amplified its reach, allowing diverse voices to converge under the banner of "wokeness." This virtual gathering of minds fostered a sense of solidarity and provided a platform for previously marginalized perspectives.

As "woke" embraced an ever-expanding array of causes, some questioned its potential dilution. Critics argued that its widespread use risked trivializing its original intent, rendering it a hollow buzzword devoid of substance. However, others saw its adaptability as a testament to its enduring power as a unifying force. The transformation of "woke" into an inclusive symbol of activism reflects the dynamism of language and its ability to transcend borders and unite humanity in the pursuit of justice and equality. As we delve into the labyrinth of "wokeness," we must recognize the potency of its evolution and its potential to inspire collective action across the vast tapestry of global struggles for social change.

## The Rise of Corporate Co-optation

Social movements and activism have become valuable commodities, ripe for exploitation by profit-driven entities in the age of consumer capitalism. As "wokeness" gained traction as a symbol of social consciousness and justice, it also caught the attention of corporate America. Seizing the opportunity to bolster their brand image and appeal to socially conscious consumers, corporations embarked on a journey of co-optation, blurring the lines between genuine activism and marketing strategy.

As the language of social justice permeated public discourse, corporations recognized its potential to resonate with consumers, especially the younger generations known for their heightened social awareness. Recognizing that being "woke" was more than just a buzzword, they sought to embrace the ethos of social consciousness to stay relevant in an evolving marketplace.

While some corporations genuinely embraced social justice issues and sought to be a force for good, others engaged in a more calculated form of activism known as "woke-washing." By co-opting the language of social justice, corporations could present a façade of virtue while continuing questionable business practices. This phenomenon, driven by profit motives rather than genuine commitment, raised ethical questions about the true intentions behind corporate "wokeness."

The rise of corporate co-optation gave rise to debates surrounding the authenticity of corporate activism. Critics argued that such endeavors were mere performance, designed to appeal to progressive consumers without any substantive commitment to social change. They expressed concern that this form of "wokeness" risked diluting the potency of genuine social justice movements, turning them into tools for corporate gain.

On the other hand, advocates of corporate social responsibility contended that engaging with social issues, even for branding purposes, could lead to positive change. They believed that corporations, as influential actors in society, could use their resources and platforms to address real-world problems effectively.

The rise of corporate co-optation of "wokeness" presents a complex conundrum, as it intertwines notions of social justice and consumer capitalism. The tension between profit motives and authentic social change underscores the need for critical evaluation of corporate activism. As we navigate the landscape of corporate "wokeness," it is essential to examine the impact of these endeavors on genuine activism and to maintain vigilance against the risk of superficial virtue signaling.

### The Woke Industrial Complex

As corporations co-opted the language of social justice, a complex web of interests emerged, blurring the lines between genuine activism and profit-driven endeavors. This intertwining of corporate interests and social justice issues gave rise to what some have called the "Woke Industrial Complex," a phenomenon where the pursuit of profit converges with the aspirations of social change, often with questionable consequences.

The Woke Industrial Complex represents the entanglement of corporate entities, media outlets, influencers, and activists, all seeking to benefit from the growing demand for "wokeness." Within this intricate system, corporations leverage social justice language to cultivate an image of social responsibility, while activists may find themselves navigating the challenges of working with profit-driven entities.

As social justice issues became marketable commodities, a dichotomy emerged between the pursuit of genuine change and the pursuit of profits. This transformation saw the monetization of activism, where slogans and symbols became branding tools. The quest for authenticity and meaningful impact often clashed with the need for corporations to protect their bottom line.

The commercialization of "wokeness" raised concerns about the impact on grassroots activism. As corporate entities redirected attention and resources towards their profit-driven agendas, there was a risk of sidelining authentic activists and community-led initiatives. The voices of marginalized communities and their lived experiences could be overshadowed by corporate messaging, undermining the essence of social justice movements.

Critics of the Woke Industrial Complex argue that the commercialization of activism commodifies social justice causes, diluting their potency and leading to superficial and performative gestures rather than substantive change. The complex interplay between corporate interests and social justice also brought attention to issues of transparency, accountability, and the need for ethical standards in corporate activism.

On the other hand, some proponents argue that the Woke Industrial Complex presents an opportunity to bring social justice issues to a broader audience and mobilize resources for positive change. They contend that corporations have the potential to use their influence, reach, and financial power to contribute to meaningful social impact if their intentions are genuinely aligned with social justice goals.

Navigating the terrain of the Woke Industrial Complex requires a critical eye and an understanding of the intricate dynamics at play. As we delve deeper into this phenomenon, it becomes evident that striking a balance between activism and commercial interests is crucial in preserving the integrity and impact of social justice movements.

## The Weaponization of "Woke"

As the term "woke" gained prominence and cultural significance, it also became a battleground for ideological warfare. The weaponization of "woke" refers to its appropriation by an extreme arm of the conservative party, transforming the term into a rhetorical weapon aimed at discrediting and undermining progressive movements and social justice causes.

The conservative misappropriation of "woke" took root as a response to the growing influence of progressive movements and their calls for systemic change. Identifying "wokeness" as a powerful symbol of social and political awakening, the extreme arm of the conservative party strategically seized the term to frame progressive ideas as radical and divisive.

By framing "woke" as a threat, the conservative weaponization of the term served to galvanize support among their base. It painted progressive activists as ideologically extreme and out of touch with mainstream values, creating a narrative of cultural division and "cancel culture."

The weaponization of "woke" relied heavily on linguistic manipulation and framing. By controlling the narrative surrounding the term, conservative forces sought to control public perception and undermine the legitimacy of social justice movements. This misuse of language served to divert attention away from substantive issues and distort the true meaning of "wokeness."

The weaponization of "woke" represents an attempt to undermine the credibility and goals of progressive movements. By framing "wokeness" as a threat to traditional values and societal cohesion, the conservative extreme positioned themselves as defenders of a purportedly embattled status quo. This strategic misuse of language has the potential to shape public opinion and stifle meaningful dialogue on critical social issues.

Critics of the conservative weaponization of "woke" argue that it perpetuates a false dichotomy, reducing complex social justice issues to mere culture wars. It diverts attention away from addressing systemic problems, perpetuating inequalities, and reinforcing oppressive structures. In doing so, the weaponization of "woke" perpetuates a cycle of division and undermines genuine efforts to create a more just and equitable society.

As we confront the weaponization of "woke," it is essential to interrogate the motives behind the misuse of language and to engage in nuanced discussions about the complex issues at the heart of social justice movements. Only by dismantling the rhetorical weapons employed against progressive causes can we foster meaningful dialogue and effect substantive change.

## Unpacking Structural Racism

At the heart of the cultural hijacking of "woke" lies a deeper, systemic issue – structural racism. Unraveling the layers of structural racism is essential to understanding how a term rooted in African American activism became a tool for ideological manipulation and cultural appropriation.

Structural racism is not an isolated phenomenon but an enduring legacy of historical oppression and systemic discrimination. From the era of slavery to the Jim Crow laws, racial biases have been deeply ingrained in institutions and societal norms. Despite progress towards racial equality, the vestiges of this historical context persist, shaping the discourse around "wokeness" and perpetuating power imbalances.

The structural racism ingrained in society provides fertile ground for cultural appropriation. The power dynamics inherent in a predominantly white society allowed for the co-optation of "woke" by conservative forces. By manipulating language and framing the term as divisive, they sought to undermine the legitimacy of social justice movements advocating for racial equity.

Cultural hijacking goes beyond mere linguistic appropriation; it reflects a broader struggle for control over narratives and cultural symbols. The redefinition of "woke" exemplifies the battle for meaning and how language can be deployed to maintain and reinforce power structures. Such actions have significant consequences, perpetuating misrepresentation and obscuring the historical and cultural significance of the term.

Unpacking structural racism requires a commitment to confronting uncomfortable truths and acknowledging the deeply rooted injustices that shape our society. It demands that we recognize how racism informs language, culture, and power dynamics, leading to the co-optation and distortion of cultural symbols like "woke."

Critically analyzing the intersection of structural racism and the cultural hijacking of "woke" allows us to challenge the narrative propagated by conservative forces. By understanding the historical context and implications of linguistic manipulation, we can work towards dismantling oppressive systems and fostering genuine dialogue on social justice issues. Only through this process of unpacking and unlearning can we hope to reclaim the essence of "woke" and steer it back towards its original call for awakening, justice, and change.

## The Quest for Authenticity

As the term "woke" traversed cultural landscapes and faced co-optation, the quest for authenticity emerged as a vital aspect of social justice movements. Distinguishing genuine activism from performative allyship became essential to preserving the integrity of causes and ensuring meaningful progress.

Authentic social justice efforts arise from a genuine commitment to address systemic issues and effect positive change. They involve actively challenging oppressive systems, amplifying marginalized voices, and engaging in allyship that centers on the needs and experiences of affected communities. On the other hand, performative allyship entails surface-level actions, often for the sake of appearances or personal gain, without a substantive commitment to dismantling systemic oppression.

As corporations embraced "wokeness" for branding purposes, the authenticity of their activism came under scrutiny. Some corporations engaged in genuine efforts to address social issues by aligning their actions with their stated values. Others, however, merely adopted the language of social justice to enhance their public image without making significant contributions to substantive change.

For activists and allies alike, the quest for authenticity poses challenges. Activists must remain steadfast in their commitment to the cause, resisting the allure of performative gestures that may lead to a hollow sense of achievement. Allies, whether individuals or corporations, must engage with humility and a willingness to learn from those most impacted by injustices. Striking a balance between authentic allyship and avoiding tokenism requires ongoing introspection and genuine dedication to learning and unlearning.

The focus must shift from performative acts to meaningful action. Genuine activism requires a deep understanding of the root causes of social issues and an unwavering commitment to addressing them. It necessitates a willingness to listen to the voices of marginalized communities and center their experiences in the fight for justice. Authenticity involves acknowledging the privilege and power one holds and using it responsibly to dismantle oppressive systems.

As we navigate the complexities of authenticity in social justice movements, transparency and accountability become guiding principles. Only through sincere engagement, critical self-reflection, and a commitment to lasting change can we ensure that "wokeness" remains grounded in genuine activism, impervious to the tides of performative virtue signaling.

### Challenging the Conservative Misappropriation

The conservative misappropriation of "woke" represents a deliberate effort to manipulate language for ideological gain. However, challenging this misrepresentation is essential to reclaiming the true meaning of "woke" and preventing its distortion from derailing genuine social justice efforts.

The misappropriation of "woke" is deeply entangled in the ideological clash between progressive and conservative forces. While progressives embrace "wokeness" as a symbol of social consciousness and justice, conservatives strategically reframe the term to cast it as a symbol of radicalism and division. This ideological battle over language shapes public perception and influences political discourse.

The conservative misappropriation of "woke" contributes to a polarized and contentious public discourse. By portraying progressive movements as extreme and out of touch, this manipulation fosters an environment of distrust and animosity between ideological camps.

This misrepresentation also distracts from the substantive issues at hand, diverting attention from the urgent need to address systemic injustices.

The conservative misuse of "woke" as a weapon serves to delegitimize progressive activists and their demands for change. By casting "wokeness" as a threat, conservatives seek to undermine the credibility of social justice movements, framing them as dangerous and divisive. This strategic use of language fosters fear and fosters an environment in which genuine dialogue and cooperation become increasingly challenging.

Challenging the conservative misappropriation of "woke" requires a commitment to truth and a refusal to be swayed by rhetorical manipulations. It involves engaging in critical analysis of the motives and narratives employed by conservative forces, while reaffirming the core principles of social justice movements. By staying grounded in the values of empathy, inclusivity, and intersectionality, advocates of genuine "wokeness" can resist attempts to tarnish its significance and redirect the conversation towards meaningful change.

It is crucial to elevate voices that challenge misrepresentations and offer nuanced perspectives. Transparent and accurate communication becomes a potent tool in dispelling misconceptions and reclaiming the narrative. By recognizing the ideological dimensions at play and holding actors accountable for their rhetoric, we can foster an environment that nurtures authentic social justice advocacy and dismantles the weaponization of "wokeness."

## The Danger of Empty Signifiers

Empty signifiers are linguistic constructs that carry significant emotional weight but lack specific, substantive meaning. In the context of "wokeness," the term's transformation into an empty signifier poses inherent dangers as it fuels misunderstanding, obfuscates complex issues, and impedes meaningful discussions about social justice and structural change.

Empty signifiers are linguistic tools that often hold multiple, contradictory interpretations, making them susceptible to manipulation and exploitation. As the term "woke" evolved and became a cultural touchstone, it also began to embody divergent meanings, becoming a vessel for projecting diverse ideological agendas.

The emotional resonance of "wokeness" is a double-edged sword. Its vagueness and adaptability allow individuals from various backgrounds to imbue the term with personal significance. Still, its malleability also creates opportunities for it to be hollowed out, becoming a mere placeholder for individual biases or political agendas.

As "wokeness" becomes increasingly divorced from its original roots and gains popularity as an empty signifier, it loses its ability to convey specific and substantive issues of social justice. This erosion of meaning enables detractors to twist the term to discredit social justice movements or ascribe radical ideologies to it, impeding productive dialogue and understanding.

The danger of empty signifiers lies in their potential to polarize discourse and divert attention from the real issues at hand. The oversimplification of complex social justice problems diminishes the urgency for comprehensive, systemic change. This phenomenon also fosters an environment where ideological divisiveness takes precedence over empathetic engagement and genuine understanding.

Addressing the danger of empty signifiers requires a commitment to fostering nuanced discussions. It is essential to reclaim the specificity of terms like "wokeness" by grounding them in their historical and cultural contexts. By acknowledging the multi-layered dimensions of social justice issues, we can resist the temptation to rely on oversimplified buzzwords, thus ensuring that substantive conversations about inequality, racism, and injustice remain at the forefront of the discourse.

As we navigate the perilous terrain of empty signifiers, it is vital to maintain vigilance against their corrosive effects on meaningful communication. By prioritizing clarity, context, and empathy, we can reinvigorate dialogue on social justice, dismantling the empty signifiers that threaten to obscure our shared pursuit of a more just and equitable world.

## Reclaiming the Narrative

As "wokeness" becomes entangled in ideological battles and subjected to cultural hijacking, reclaiming the narrative becomes imperative to safeguard its true meaning and redirect its focus back to substantive social justice issues. Reclamation involves wresting the term from the clutches of misrepresentation, empowering marginalized voices, and nurturing genuine cross-cultural understanding.

The battle for the meaning of "woke" can distract from the pressing social justice issues that originally defined the term. Reclaiming the narrative requires redirecting the conversation towards structural inequalities, systemic racism, economic disparities, and other substantive matters that demand urgent attention and action.

The co-optation of "woke" by far right conservative forces and corporate interests can foster division and misunderstanding. Reclamation involves fostering cross-cultural understanding and empathy, transcending the barriers created by misappropriation. By acknowledging the diverse perspectives and experiences of different communities, we can forge solidarity and a shared commitment to change.

Reclaiming the narrative requires deliberate strategies to wrest the term "woke" from its misappropriation. This may involve amplifying the voices of activists and marginalized communities, engaging in public education about the term's historical roots, and promoting honest and nuanced discussions about its implications.

Central to the process of reclamation is elevating authentic social justice activism over performative gestures. By demonstrating the tangible impact of genuine efforts towards a more equitable society, the true meaning of "woke" can be revitalized, setting it on a course aligned with its historical roots and initial intent.

To reclaim the narrative, it is essential to transcend ideological barriers and work towards a shared understanding of the complexities of social justice issues. Empowering marginalized voices and centering the experiences of affected communities in discussions about "wokeness" fosters a more inclusive and transformative dialogue.

By challenging the divisive forces that have manipulated and distorted the term, we can steer the conversation back towards substantive change. Reclaiming the narrative surrounding "wokeness" is a collective endeavor, requiring openness, empathy, and a renewed commitment to fostering a more just and equitable society for all.

## Towards a Genuine Awakening

In the quest to reclaim the true essence of "wokeness," the journey towards a genuine awakening beckons. This awakening involves a profound commitment to understanding the struggles faced by marginalized communities, dismantling systemic inequalities, and effecting meaningful societal change rooted in empathy, compassion, and solidarity.

Genuine awakening begins with individual self-reflection and recognition of the privileges and biases that shape our perspectives. By acknowledging our role in perpetuating inequality, we can embark on a path of unlearning and challenging oppressive structures. Collectively, this responsibility extends to communities and institutions, fostering a sense of accountability in advancing justice for all.

True awakening requires actively seeking to understand the lived experiences of marginalized communities and centering their voices in discussions about their own challenges and aspirations. By actively listening to their stories, we can foster empathy and solidarity, recognizing that the pursuit of justice is interconnected with the liberation of all.

Genuine awakening is not a fleeting moment of realization but an ongoing commitment to social change. It involves sustained efforts to challenge oppressive systems, address structural racism, and advocate for policies that uplift marginalized communities. This commitment must extend beyond performative gestures, transcending political trends and commercial interests.

As we journey towards a genuine awakening, we must navigate the complexities of language and remain vigilant against empty signifiers and ideological manipulations. By refocusing our energy on substantive issues and genuine allyship, we can reclaim the narrative surrounding "wokeness" and redefine it as a powerful force for transformative change.

True awakening embraces the interconnectedness of struggles for justice, recognizing that no social justice cause exists in isolation. By fostering intersectionality in activism, we can forge strong alliances, harness collective power, and drive change across diverse communities.

The path towards a genuine awakening involves collective introspection, empathy, and a steadfast commitment to dismantling oppressive systems. It demands that we confront the dangers of linguistic manipulation and cultural appropriation, redirecting our focus towards addressing the pressing social justice issues that define the core of "wokeness." By reclaiming the true meaning of "woke" and embodying its spirit in our actions, we can forge a more just and equitable society for all.

*"Misusing 'woke' is like painting over truth with the colors of pretentiousness."*

# CHAPTER 1
# AWAKENING ORIGINS

Certain words carry profound historical significance, encapsulating the struggles, aspirations, and transformative potential of social movements. "Woke" is one such term, whose journey from its humble origins in African American Vernacular English (AAVE) to its current status as a symbol of social consciousness and justice represents a powerful narrative of awakening and activism. In this chapter, we delve into the historical origins of "wokeness," unearthing its roots within the civil rights and Black liberation movements of the 20th century and exploring how it has evolved into the multifaceted concept we know today.

The term "stay woke" first emerged in AAVE, a unique dialect rich in cultural significance within African American communities. It carried an urgent call to remain vigilant and aware of the systemic injustices that plagued society. Originating from gospel and blues traditions, the phrase served as a reminder to stay awake both spiritually and politically, resisting complacency in the face of racial oppression.

As the civil rights movement gained momentum in the mid-20th century, "stay woke" became emblematic of the struggle for racial equality. It resonated with activists who fought tirelessly for justice, empowering them to challenge the status quo and demand systemic change. The phrase encapsulated a state of awakened consciousness, transcending mere awareness to mobilize action against discrimination and inequality.

Over time, "stay woke" underwent a transformation, shedding its original form to become the more concise "woke." This evolution allowed the term to expand its scope beyond its historical roots while maintaining its essence of social awakening. "Woke" became a versatile term, embracing various social justice causes, each fueled by a commitment to challenging injustice and fostering positive change.

Within the civil rights and Black liberation movements, being "woke" was not just a descriptive label; it embodied a profound philosophy of activism. To be "woke" meant engaging in the continuous pursuit of justice and equity, reflecting a deep sense of empathy and solidarity with marginalized communities. It signified a willingness to confront uncomfortable truths, challenge systemic racism, and work tirelessly towards a more equitable society.

The power of "wokeness" as a language of social awakening lies in its ability to inspire collective action and mobilize communities around shared values. This transformative force of language extends beyond its lexical meaning; it resonates with a broader narrative of resistance and resilience, highlighting the struggles and triumphs of marginalized communities throughout history.

"Wokeness" has become a rallying cry for advocates of change, transcending geographical boundaries and linguistic barriers. It has found new life in the digital age, amplified by social media platforms, where it can galvanize global solidarity and draw attention to pressing issues. This chapter seeks to explore the rich historical tapestry of "wokeness" and its evolution as a symbol of activism and social consciousness.

By unearthing its roots in AAVE and tracing its trajectory through the civil rights and Black liberation movements, we gain insights into the term's profound significance and the struggles it represents. As we delve into the awakening origins of "wokeness," we recognize the potential for language to shape societal consciousness and inspire transformative change.

## The Birth of "Stay Woke"

The roots of "wokeness" lie deeply embedded in the vibrant tapestry of AAVE. From the spirituals of the enslaved to the protest songs of the civil rights era, the language served as a powerful tool of resistance and cultural expression within African American communities. Central to this linguistic landscape was the phrase "stay woke," whose genesis emerged from the historical crucible of oppression and resilience.

The term "stay woke" originated in African American communities as a colloquial expression of vigilance and alertness. Dating back to the 19th century, the phrase was intertwined with the struggle for freedom and dignity in the face of racial injustice. Slaves would caution one another to "stay woke" during secret gatherings, reminding each other to remain vigilant against slaveholders' surveillance and exploitation.

As the African American experience evolved, so did the phrase "stay woke," gaining prominence during the civil rights movement of the 1960s. It became a rallying cry for activists and organizers, embodying a fervent call to remain vigilant against the systemic oppression that had subjugated African Americans for generations. From the pulpits of Black churches to the podiums of civil rights leaders, "stay woke" echoed through the streets of America's struggle for racial equality.

The essence of "stay woke" transcended mere wakefulness; it signified a state of heightened awareness and consciousness. Being "woke" meant recognizing and challenging the deep-seated prejudices and structures that perpetuated racial inequality. This state of awakening was not just a solitary journey but a collective responsibility to resist complacency and actively pursue social change.

Within the lexicon of AAVE, "stay woke" also conveyed spiritual undertones. The concept of staying awake took on a metaphorical meaning, urging individuals to remain spiritually attuned to the struggle for justice. It became a symbol of the spiritual awakening needed to confront the moral and ethical contradictions that underpinned a society divided by race.

As the civil rights movement gained momentum, "stay woke" reverberated through protest songs and the oratory of leaders like Malcolm X and Stokely Carmichael. The phrase became synonymous with the fight for civil rights and racial dignity, inspiring generations of activists who understood that the struggle for justice required vigilance and unwavering commitment.

Over time, "stay woke" began to transcend its immediate context, resonating with diverse communities and social justice causes. Beyond its African American roots, the phrase embodied a universal ethos of resistance and awareness. It crossed cultural boundaries to address broader issues of systemic oppression, racism, and social inequality.

The transformation of "stay woke" into the more succinct "woke" reflected the linguistic dynamism inherent in the evolution of language. As language adapts to changing contexts, it sheds elements while retaining its essence. "Woke" emerged as a concise yet potent expression of social consciousness, imbued with the historical weight of the struggle for justice.

The birth of "stay woke" as a call to remain vigilant against injustice represents a powerful legacy of linguistic resilience within African American culture. Its evolution from the clandestine gatherings of enslaved individuals to the rallying cry of civil rights activists illustrates how language can become a vessel for collective memory and the preservation of cultural identity.

Continuing these thoughts, we venture deeper into the transformation of "woke" and its expansion into a broader symbol of social consciousness. As we trace its journey from a localized expression to a global movement, we confront the challenges posed by co-optation and the weaponization of "wokeness." By grounding ourselves in its historical origins, we equip ourselves with the understanding needed to navigate the complexities of reclaiming the narrative surrounding "wokeness" and its vital role in contemporary social justice movements.

## The Evolution of "Wokeness"

As the civil rights movement ushered in significant changes in American society, the phrase "stay woke" continued to reverberate, resonating with a generation committed to challenging systemic racism and promoting social justice. The transformation of "stay woke" into the more succinct "woke" marked a pivotal moment in the evolution of the term, as it transcended its historical roots to encompass a broader range of social justice causes.

The 1970s saw the emergence of "woke" as a descriptor within African American communities, expanding beyond its original context as a call to action. In this new form, being "woke" denoted an individual's heightened awareness of social inequalities and a commitment to confronting them. It was an assertion of identity and consciousness, reflecting the ongoing struggle for racial equality.

As the civil rights era gave way to the post-civil rights era, the concept of "wokeness" continued to evolve. The 1980s and 1990s witnessed a resurgence of Black activism and cultural expression, with hip-hop becoming a powerful medium for voicing social and political concerns. Within the hip-hop community, "stay woke" and later "woke" became recurrent themes in songs and lyrics, reinforcing the term's connection to social justice and Black empowerment.

The advent of the internet and social media in the late 20th and early 21st centuries facilitated the rapid dissemination of ideas and language. "Woke" found new life as an easily shareable term, quickly permeating various online platforms and digital conversations. Its use expanded beyond African American communities, transcending cultural and geographical boundaries.

The multifaceted nature of "wokeness" allowed the term to encompass a range of social justice causes. It became a unifying symbol for various movements, including feminism, LGBTQ+ rights, environmental justice, and more. Embracing "wokeness" as a shared identity, activists found common ground in their pursuit of justice and equity, regardless of their specific causes.

However, the term's increasing popularity also presented challenges. As "wokeness" entered mainstream discourse, it risked dilution and misappropriation. Its evolving meanings became subject to interpretation, leaving room for misunderstandings and the potential for co-optation by those seeking to exploit its popularity for personal or political gain.

The transition from "stay woke" to "woke" signified more than just linguistic brevity; it represented a shifting focus from individual vigilance to collective awareness. The evolution of the term mirrored the broader trajectory of social justice movements, which transitioned from the civil rights era's emphasis on legal desegregation to the contemporary pursuit of dismantling systemic inequalities.

With this evolution came the acknowledgement that "wokeness" encompassed both self-awareness and systemic analysis. It encouraged individuals not only to confront their biases and privilege but also to understand how systemic racism, discrimination, and oppression perpetuated social inequalities. "Wokeness" became a call to action to challenge both personal prejudices and the institutional barriers that hindered progress.

The expansion of "wokeness" beyond its original context demonstrated its adaptability and relevance in an ever-changing world. As issues of social justice evolved, so did the term, embracing the complexity and intersectionality of modern activism.

As we go further, we explore how "wokeness" became a cultural touchstone for social justice movements and the dangers it faced as it garnered popularity. By delving into the implications of its transformation into a symbol of activism, we gain a deeper understanding of the challenges in navigating the contemporary landscape of "wokeness." Ultimately, we seek to reclaim the term's true meaning and its potential as a force for genuine awakening and transformative change.

## Awakening as a Philosophy

Beyond its linguistic significance, "wokeness" emerged as a powerful philosophy within the civil rights and Black liberation movements. It represented more than just a state of heightened awareness; it encapsulated a profound commitment to challenging oppressive systems, pursuing justice, and effecting transformative change. "Wokeness" as a philosophy embodied the essence of social consciousness and activism, reflecting the struggles and aspirations of marginalized communities throughout history.

At the heart of "wokeness" as a philosophy was the notion of awakened consciousness. To be "woke" was to acknowledge the interconnectedness of social injustices and to understand that no struggle for justice occurred in isolation. The civil rights era provided a backdrop for the realization that the fight for racial equality was linked to broader efforts to combat poverty, gender discrimination, and other forms of systemic oppression.

The philosophy of "wokeness" also emphasized the role of empathy and solidarity in activism. It encouraged individuals to engage with the experiences and struggles of others, recognizing that the pursuit of justice was a collective endeavor. This sense of shared responsibility fostered alliances between diverse communities, reinforcing the understanding that social change required a united front.

The struggle for justice inherent in "wokeness" was not confined to the pursuit of legal rights or superficial change. It went beyond superficial fixes to address the underlying structures and root causes of systemic injustice. "Wokeness" encouraged a commitment to dismantling oppressive systems, advocating for policies that uplifted marginalized communities, and fostering genuine empathy and understanding.

Within African American communities, "wokeness" also held spiritual significance. The call to "stay woke" during times of slavery symbolized the need to remain spiritually alert and attuned to the divine in the face of hardship. As the civil rights movement drew upon religious imagery and language, the concept of being "woke" became synonymous with the spiritual awakening needed to confront social and moral contradictions.

The philosophy of "wokeness" also encompassed self-awareness and critical reflection. It urged individuals to confront their own biases, prejudices, and privileges, recognizing that dismantling systemic racism required a commitment to challenging personal prejudices as well. "Wokeness" encouraged the unlearning of harmful ideologies and a willingness to engage in ongoing self-education and growth.

Moreover, the philosophy of "wokeness" understood that activism was not a singular event but an ongoing journey. It acknowledged that progress towards justice was gradual, requiring sustained efforts and resilience in the face of setbacks. This acknowledgment of the long-term nature of social change tempered the desire for quick fixes, emphasizing the importance of perseverance and community support.

As "wokeness" evolved from the civil rights era to the present, its philosophical essence remained intact. It continued to inspire activists and advocates for social justice, transcending its historical context to become a guiding principle for diverse movements worldwide. Beyond being a mere term, "wokeness" embodied a way of being – one that demanded introspection, collective responsibility, and a commitment to dismantling oppressive structures.

As we move ahead, we discover how "wokeness" as a philosophy influenced contemporary social justice movements. We explore the implications of its transformation into a global symbol of activism, navigating the challenges posed by its co-optation and misappropriation. By reclaiming the philosophical underpinnings of "wokeness," we endeavor to foster a more genuine understanding of the term's power to awaken consciousness, inspire transformative change, and drive us towards a more just and equitable society for all.

## The Language of Social Awakening

Language has always played a pivotal role in shaping social movements and cultural discourse. Within the context of "wokeness," language served as a potent tool of social awakening, igniting a collective consciousness and inspiring activism against systemic injustices. The evolution of "wokeness" from a localized expression to a global phenomenon was facilitated, in part, by its resonance as a language of social awakening.

Language possesses the power to evoke emotions, convey complex ideas, and unite diverse communities. In the civil rights era, the phrase "stay woke" embodied these attributes, encapsulating the urgency of the struggle for racial equality. Its cultural and historical significance imbued it with a deep emotional resonance, transforming it from a mere colloquialism into a rallying cry for justice.

The language of "stay woke" carried the weight of history and the wisdom of generations of resilience. It transcended its immediate context, echoing the struggles of oppressed communities worldwide and connecting with the broader human experience of resistance and liberation. This linguistic universality allowed "wokeness" to transcend geographical and cultural boundaries, resonating with marginalized groups across the globe.

As "stay woke" evolved into "woke," its brevity and versatility rendered it easily shareable in the digital age. Social media platforms became vehicles for the dissemination of "wokeness," enabling individuals to connect, share information, and mobilize collective action. The power of language in shaping narratives and mobilizing communities manifested itself in the viral spread of "woke" as a symbol of social consciousness.

With its newfound digital presence, "wokeness" also faced the risk of dilution and misappropriation. The speed at which language spreads in the digital realm can lead to superficial understandings of complex issues. "Wokeness" became susceptible to being co-opted by performative activism, where gestures were more about appearances than genuine commitment to change. The very platforms that amplified its message could also distort its meaning.

However, the adaptability of "wokeness" as a language of social awakening also enabled it to bridge gaps between different movements. The shared identity of being "woke" united activists across various social justice causes, fostering connections between advocates for racial justice, gender equality, LGBTQ+ rights, environmental sustainability, and more. This interconnectedness demonstrated the power of language in forging alliances and advancing collective goals.

Beyond its linguistic fluidity, the language of "wokeness" encouraged a deeper understanding of intersecting oppressions. The philosophy of "wokeness" emphasized the need to recognize the interconnectedness of struggles against racism, sexism, homophobia, transphobia, ableism, and other forms of discrimination. Language acted as a vehicle to elevate these conversations, creating spaces for intersectional analysis and inclusive activism.

The language of "wokeness" also facilitated conversations about privilege and allyship. Advocates of "wokeness" recognized the importance of individuals using their positions of privilege to uplift marginalized voices and effect change. Language allowed for the recognition and acknowledgment of privilege as a step towards more inclusive and effective activism.

As the term "wokeness" gained prominence in popular culture, it faced both acclaim and criticism. Some celebrated its potential to awaken societal consciousness and foster positive change, while others derided it as a mere buzzword devoid of substantive impact. This duality underscored the complexities of language as a tool of social awakening, as it could be embraced, contested, and co-opted simultaneously.

Next, we'll examine how the language of "wokeness" became a cultural touchstone for social justice movements. We navigate the challenges posed by its co-optation and the weaponization of "wokeness." By examining the complexities of its transformation into a symbol of activism, we strive to reclaim its true meaning as a force for genuine awakening and transformative change. The power of language in shaping societal consciousness remains a potent force, capable of inspiring collective action and driving us towards a more just and equitable world.

## The Quest for Justice

At the heart of "wokeness" lies an unwavering commitment to justice – a quest that has animated social justice movements throughout history. The evolution of the term from "stay woke" to "woke" mirrored the broader trajectory of the civil rights and Black liberation movements. This explores how the concept of "wokeness" became synonymous with the pursuit of justice and how it continues to guide contemporary social justice endeavors.

The civil rights era was a defining moment in American history, marked by fierce resistance against racial segregation and discrimination. The philosophy of "stay woke" embedded within it a fervent determination to seek justice for African Americans who had endured centuries of oppression. The struggle for justice went beyond legal desegregation; it encompassed the fight for economic equality, political representation, and the recognition of the humanity and dignity of Black individuals.

As the term "stay woke" evolved into "woke," its association with justice deepened. "Wokeness" became a philosophy of awakening to the broader web of systemic oppressions that plagued society. It encouraged individuals to connect the dots between various forms of discrimination and to recognize that justice was intrinsically interconnected across different marginalized communities.

The quest for justice went beyond singular demands for individual rights; it entailed challenging the very structures that perpetuated inequality. The civil rights movement sought to dismantle Jim Crow laws and segregation, but it also aimed to address the root causes of racial disparities in housing, education, employment, and criminal justice.

The philosophy of "wokeness" emphasized the necessity of empathy and solidarity in the quest for justice. It encouraged activists to bridge divides and recognize the common humanity shared by all people. "Wokeness" aspired to build alliances between diverse communities, recognizing that the fight for justice required collective effort.

As the civil rights movement transitioned into the post-civil rights era, the quest for justice expanded beyond racial equality. Movements for gender equality, LGBTQ+ rights, disability rights, and environmental justice found common cause in the broader philosophy of "wokeness." The pursuit of justice became an intersectional endeavor, recognizing that oppressions intersected in complex ways and must be addressed collectively.

The language of "wokeness" facilitated conversations about privilege and power, pushing individuals to confront their own biases and positions of advantage. Recognizing privilege was not an exercise in guilt but a call to action. "Wokeness" encouraged those with privilege to use it responsibly, advocating for justice and amplifying marginalized voices.

With its digital dissemination, "wokeness" gained visibility and momentum in the contemporary world. It found resonance in the age of social media, where stories of injustice could reach millions in a matter of seconds. The language of "wokeness" became a rallying cry for those seeking justice and a tool to hold institutions accountable.

However, as the term "wokeness" entered mainstream discourse, it faced challenges. Its growing popularity led to concerns of performative activism, where gestures were superficial without substantive action. Co-optation by corporations and political interests further diluted its meaning, leading to accusations of "woke-washing" – using social justice language for marketing or political purposes without enacting real change.

Yet, the core philosophy of "wokeness" endured, inspiring genuine activists committed to the quest for justice. It remained a powerful force for societal transformation, driving the fight for equity, inclusivity, and systemic change.

As you continue, we explore the challenges posed by the co-optation and weaponization of "wokeness." By examining the implications of its transformation into a global symbol of activism, we aim to reclaim its true meaning and its potential as a force for genuine awakening and transformative change. The quest for justice remains at the heart of "wokeness," guiding us towards a more just and equitable world where the struggle for justice transcends linguistic boundaries.

The journey of "wokeness" from its humble origins in AAVE to its current status as a symbol of social consciousness and justice is a powerful narrative of awakening and activism. Rooted in the civil rights and Black liberation movements, "wokeness" emerged as a call to remain vigilant against systemic injustices, transcending its original context to encompass a broader philosophy of social awakening.

The historical significance of "stay woke" lies in its role as a secret code among enslaved individuals, warning each other to remain alert and vigilant against oppressive forces. As the civil rights era unfolded, the phrase gained momentum, becoming emblematic of the struggle for racial equality and justice. Its transformation into the more succinct "woke" marked a pivotal moment, signifying the shift from individual vigilance to collective awareness.

As "wokeness" evolved, it embraced a multifaceted identity that resonated with diverse social justice causes. Its philosophy centered on awakened consciousness, interconnected struggles for justice, empathy, and the dismantling of oppressive structures. "Wokeness" united activists across different movements, forging alliances and recognizing the need for collective action.

The language of "wokeness" played a critical role in shaping its spread and impact. From the civil rights era to the digital age, language acted as a potent tool of social awakening. The phrase "stay woke" carried the weight of history and the wisdom of generations, transcending cultural and geographical boundaries. In the digital era, the term "woke" gained traction through social media, spreading its message of social consciousness rapidly.

However, the rapid dissemination of "wokeness" also introduced challenges. Its increasing popularity led to concerns about performative activism, where gestures were superficial without substantive action. Co-optation and "woke-washing" by corporations and political interests risked diluting the term's true meaning, leading to accusations of exploitation for profit or political gain.

The language of "wokeness" served as a rallying cry for marginalized communities worldwide. It bridged divides, encouraging intersectional analyses of oppressions and promoting dialogue about privilege and power. It inspired individuals to confront their biases and embrace the collective responsibility for social change.

As we navigate the complexities of reclaiming the true essence of "wokeness," it is crucial to remember its historical roots  and the struggles it represents. The quest for justice lies at the heart of "wokeness," driving us towards a more just and equitable society. Acknowledging the dangers of misappropriation, we must resist the commodification of "wokeness" and remain vigilant against performative gestures that lack substantive impact.

To foster a more genuine awakening, we must prioritize substantive action and allyship. "Wokeness" demands ongoing self-reflection, education, and a commitment to dismantling systemic oppression. It encourages empathetic engagement with the struggles faced by marginalized communities and the recognition of privilege as a call to action.

The true power of "wokeness" lies in its potential to inspire transformative change. By reclaiming its narrative and guarding against co-optation, we can foster a more nuanced understanding of "wokeness" as a force for positive societal transformation.

As we embark on a journey towards genuine awakening, it is essential to recognize the interconnectedness of struggles for justice. The pursuit of racial equality, gender equity, LGBTQ+ rights, environmental sustainability, and other social justice causes must be approached as interwoven endeavors. By embracing intersectionality, we amplify the collective impact of our activism and create space for inclusive dialogue and action.

The awakening origins of "wokeness" connect us to a history of resilience, resistance, and the pursuit of justice. As we navigate the complexities of reclaiming and preserving its true meaning, we remain steadfast in our commitment to transformative change. "Wokeness" embodies a philosophy of collective consciousness, empathy, and action, inspiring us to challenge oppressive systems and advocate for a more just and equitable world. We should, all of us, remain vigilant and authentic in our pursuit of "wokeness," ensuring that its transformative potential continues to guide us towards a brighter and more inclusive future.

*"Being 'woke' used to be about tearing down walls; now it's about building walls of ignorance."*

# CHAPTER 2
# A SOCIAL REVOLUTION

We live in an ever-evolving landscape of social change and a profound shift is underway, reshaping the contours of activism, advocacy, and public discourse. This chapter introduces you to the essence of this transformation, which has come to be known as a "Social Revolution." The Social Revolution is a multifaceted phenomenon characterized by the mobilization of diverse communities, demanding justice, equity, and an end to systemic oppression. It marks a departure from traditional modes of protest and resistance, embracing innovative approaches to effect transformative change.

The Social Revolution is not confined to any specific geographic location or demographic group; instead, it is a global and intersectional movement that cuts across boundaries of race, gender, class, and nationality. At its core, this revolution is an awakening, an eruption of collective consciousness, prompting individuals and communities to question long-standing norms, challenge institutionalized discrimination, and confront the deep-seated roots of inequality.

This chapter seeks to illuminate the key dimensions and driving forces of the Social Revolution, recognizing the pivotal role of technology, culture, and interconnectedness in catalyzing and sustaining this paradigm shift. The advent of the digital age has redefined the ways in which activism is conducted, creating new avenues for mobilization and amplifying marginalized voices. Social media platforms have become powerful tools for disseminating information, organizing grassroots movements, and holding institutions accountable.

Furthermore, the Social Revolution is intrinsically tied to cultural shifts, as the concepts of identity, representation, and inclusivity take center stage. Through the embrace of intersectionality, activists and advocates recognize the interconnectedness of various forms of oppression, weaving together struggles against racism, sexism, homophobia, ableism, and other societal injustices.

In exploring the facets of this transformative movement, this chapter will examine case studies of successful social revolutions that have shaped history and paved the way for contemporary activism. From the Civil Rights Movement to the Arab Spring, these examples illustrate the immense potential of collective action in reshaping political landscapes and dismantling oppressive systems.

Throughout this chapter, we will seek to comprehend the complexities and challenges faced by the Social Revolution. The delicate balance between advocating for change and preserving the authenticity of social justice causes will be explored, as well as the tensions that arise when confronting institutional power structures. The ethical considerations and responsibilities inherent in participating in this revolution will also be examined, as the quest for justice calls for vigilance against co-optation and performative activism.

As we navigate the contours of the Social Revolution, it is crucial to recognize that this is not a momentary trend but a continuous journey towards a more just and equitable world. It demands collective resilience, empathy, and a commitment to dismantling the systems that perpetuate injustice. In the sections that follow, we will look into the multifaceted dimensions of this movement, exploring its historical foundations, its evolution in contemporary society, and the strategies employed to realize its transformative vision.

## The Digital Age: Amplifying Voices

The digital age has emerged as a powerful force in shaping the trajectory of social revolution. The advent of technology and the proliferation of social media platforms have revolutionized the way information is disseminated, movements are organized, and voices are amplified. This section delves into the impact of the digital age on the Social Revolution, exploring how it has provided a platform for marginalized voices, facilitated global solidarity, and catalyzed transformative change.

One of the most significant contributions of the digital age to the Social Revolution is the democratization of information. In the past, media channels were predominantly controlled by corporate entities, which often perpetuated mainstream narratives that marginalized certain communities and suppressed dissenting voices. However, the rise of social media has provided an alternative space for diverse perspectives to be heard, fostering a more inclusive and nuanced public discourse.

Social media platforms, such as Twitter, Facebook, Instagram, and YouTube, have become vital tools for activists and organizers to reach a broader audience. Through the use of hashtags, trending topics, and viral campaigns, social justice movements can quickly gain momentum and capture the attention of millions worldwide. The power of these platforms to amplify marginalized voices cannot be underestimated, as they enable individuals and communities to share their experiences, challenge dominant narratives, and build solidarity with like-minded advocates across the globe.

Furthermore, the digital age has transformed the way social revolutions are organized and mobilized. Online platforms have facilitated the rapid coordination of protests, marches, and demonstrations, allowing activists to synchronize their efforts across different locations and time zones. Virtual spaces have become hubs for strategic planning, resource-sharing, and the dissemination of educational materials, empowering advocates with tools to drive change.

The digital age has also challenged traditional media gatekeeping, enabling citizen journalists to report on events as they unfold. In instances of civil unrest or social upheaval, these citizen journalists play a critical role in sharing information from the frontlines, often providing perspectives that mainstream media might overlook or disregard. This direct access to information has engendered a more transparent and accountable approach to reporting, fostering an informed and engaged citizenry.

However, while the digital age has undoubtedly amplified marginalized voices and catalyzed social revolutions, it also presents its own challenges. The spread of misinformation, the echo chamber effect, and the rapid pace of digital discourse can sometimes hinder nuanced conversations and impede the pursuit of genuine understanding. Additionally, the prevalence of online harassment and digital surveillance poses risks to the safety and well-being of activists.

As we navigate the opportunities and challenges presented by the digital age, it is essential to recognize its potential to reshape the dynamics of power and representation. By leveraging technology responsibly and ethically, the Social Revolution can harness the full potential of the digital age to amplify marginalized voices, build inclusive movements, and foster a more just and equitable world.

## Intersectionality and Solidarity

At the heart of the Social Revolution lies the concept of intersectionality, which has become a guiding principle in contemporary activism. Coined by Kimberlé Crenshaw in the late 1980s, intersectionality recognizes the interconnected nature of various forms of oppression, acknowledging that individuals can experience multiple layers of marginalization based on their race, gender, class, sexuality, ability, and other identities. This section explores the significance of intersectionality in the Social Revolution, emphasizing its role in fostering solidarity, inclusivity, and transformative change.

Traditional modes of activism often focused on single-issue campaigns, addressing specific injustices in isolation. However, intersectionality challenges this fragmented approach, urging advocates to recognize and address the complex intersections of power and privilege that shape people's lives. By understanding how systems of oppression are interconnected, activists can forge alliances that bridge divides and build solidarity among diverse communities.

Intersectionality enriches the Social Revolution by creating space for voices that have historically been silenced or marginalized within social justice movements. It compels activists to center the experiences and perspectives of those most impacted by injustice, challenging dominant narratives and elevating the importance of lived experiences. Through this process, intersectionality promotes a deeper understanding of the root causes of inequality, enabling advocates to develop more effective and holistic strategies for change.

The inclusion of intersectionality also serves as a crucial countermeasure against co-optation and tokenism within the Social Revolution. By embracing a framework that values diverse identities and experiences, activists can ensure that their movements are authentically representative of the communities they seek to uplift. This commitment to inclusivity fosters a culture of trust, respect, and collaboration, vital elements in building sustainable and transformative movements.

Moreover, intersectionality provides a lens through which activists can critically analyze the ways in which privilege operates within their own ranks. Recognizing the diverse identities and experiences within their movements, activists can engage in self-reflection and ensure that their advocacy is informed by a commitment to equity and justice for all.

Intersectionality not only informs the strategies and tactics of the Social Revolution but also extends to the vision of a more just and equitable future. The pursuit of social justice is intrinsically tied to addressing the interlocking systems of oppression that shape our societies. This holistic approach calls for transformative change that dismantles the very foundations of injustice, creating space for the liberation of all individuals from oppressive systems.

Intersectionality is a powerful force in the Social Revolution, guiding activists toward more inclusive, impactful, and sustainable movements. By embracing intersectionality, the Social Revolution can transcend the limitations of single-issue activism and build coalitions that challenge the root causes of inequality. Coming up, we discuss the transformative potential of intersectional activism and the ways in which it reshapes culture, identity, and solidarity in the pursuit of justice.

## From Individual Awareness to Collective Action

The Social Revolution is a dynamic and collective endeavor that transcends individual awareness and extends into transformative collective action. While individual consciousness and self-awareness play pivotal roles in igniting the spark of change, it is the synergy of collective mobilization that propels the Social Revolution forward. This section explores the critical journey from individual awareness to collective action, emphasizing the power of solidarity and the role of grassroots movements in effecting transformative change.

Individual awareness serves as the foundational building block of the Social Revolution. It is the moment when individuals recognize the injustices that pervade society and confront their own biases and privileges. This awakening is an intimate and deeply personal process, often driven by exposure to diverse perspectives, lived experiences, and critical education. As individuals come to terms with the complex interplay of power and oppression, they are primed to move beyond passive acknowledgment to proactive engagement.

From individual awareness, a crucial transformation occurs as advocates evolve from passive observers to active agents of change. It is the pivotal point at which individual passion and conviction converge with collective aspirations for justice and equity. This transition is catalyzed by the realization that solitary actions, though powerful, are limited in scope and impact. To achieve lasting change, collective action is required.

Collective action is the lifeblood of the Social Revolution, the synergy of individual energies aligned toward shared goals. It is the embodiment of intersectionality in action, as diverse communities unite under the banner of solidarity to dismantle oppressive structures. Through collective action, the Social Revolution transcends geographic boundaries and cultural divides, connecting activists across the globe in a shared pursuit of justice.

Grassroots movements play a central role in fostering collective action. These movements emanate from the very communities most affected by injustice, empowering individuals to raise their voices, reclaim their narratives, and challenge the status quo. Grassroots activism allows for a more organic and bottom-up approach, ensuring that the movement is rooted in the needs and aspirations of those it seeks to serve.

Moreover, collective action is not confined to mass protests or large-scale demonstrations. It is also manifested in the everyday actions of individuals who commit to living out their values in their personal and professional lives. It can be seen in the decisions of consumers to support ethically conscious businesses, in the efforts of educators to incorporate diverse perspectives into their curricula, and in the commitment of allies to stand in solidarity with marginalized communities.

The Social Revolution is a collective journey that begins with individual awareness and unfolds through the power of collective action. As individuals awaken to the injustices that permeate society, they are compelled to act, uniting with others in a shared pursuit of justice, equity, and liberation. The Social Revolution thrives in grassroots movements, driven by the authentic voices of those most impacted by oppression. Moving forward, we dig deeper into the intricacies of collective action, exploring its diverse manifestations and the transformative potential it holds in shaping the trajectory of the Social Revolution.

## The Challenges of Performative Activism

As the Social Revolution gains momentum, it also faces challenges that can hinder its transformative potential. One such obstacle is the rise of performative activism, which involves individuals and organizations engaging in symbolic gestures without making substantive contributions to social change. This section explores the complexities and dangers of performative activism, emphasizing the need for authentic, accountable, and sustained advocacy.

Performative activism often manifests as superficial displays of support for social justice causes. It may involve sharing social justice slogans or hashtags on social media without actively engaging in concrete actions to address the root causes of injustice. Performative activists may seek to align themselves with popular movements as a means of enhancing their public image or gaining social capital, rather than genuinely committing to dismantling oppressive systems.

One of the challenges posed by performative activism is its potential to co-opt and dilute the goals of genuine social justice movements. As hollow gestures take the spotlight, the substantive demands of activists working toward transformative change may be sidelined or trivialized. This phenomenon can lead to the erasure of marginalized voices and the perpetuation of harmful power dynamics within the movement.

Moreover, performative activism can contribute to the commodification of social justice, where advocacy is reduced to a marketable brand rather than a commitment to social change. In this context, social justice language and symbolism may be appropriated for commercial gain, rendering them devoid of their original significance and impact.

Performative activism also faces criticism for its selective engagement with social justice causes. Some individuals and corporations may embrace certain issues while remaining silent or complicit on others, signaling a lack of genuine commitment to comprehensive systemic change. This cherry-picking of causes can undermine the solidarity necessary to address the intersectional nature of injustice effectively.

The challenges of performative activism extend beyond individual actions to encompass institutional practices. Some organizations may adopt superficial diversity and inclusion initiatives or virtue signaling without actively addressing the structural barriers that perpetuate inequality within their ranks. Such tokenistic efforts can impede meaningful progress and accountability.

To overcome the pitfalls of performative activism, it is essential to cultivate a culture of authenticity, accountability, and sustained engagement within the Social Revolution. Advocates must interrogate their motivations and actions, ensuring that their advocacy aligns with their values and principles. They should actively seek out marginalized voices and center their perspectives in decision-making processes.

Additionally, advocates should challenge and confront performative activism when they encounter it within their communities and institutions. Engaging in difficult conversations about the complexities of social change and collective responsibility is essential for the growth and resilience of the Social Revolution.

The challenges posed by performative activism demand vigilance and introspection from those engaged in the Social Revolution. The pursuit of transformative change requires authentic commitment, sustained advocacy, and accountability for individual and collective actions. By actively confronting and addressing the pitfalls of performative activism, the Social Revolution can strengthen its impact and drive meaningful progress toward a more just and equitable world.

### The Co-optation of "Wokeness"

"Wokeness" has emerged as a powerful term within the Social Revolution, signifying a heightened awareness of social injustices and a commitment to challenging oppressive systems. However, like many concepts at the forefront of social change, "wokeness" has not been immune to co-optation. This section explores the co-optation of "wokeness" and its implications for the Social Revolution, emphasizing the importance of safeguarding the integrity and authenticity of the movement.

Co-optation refers to the process by which dominant institutions or groups appropriate elements of a social movement for their benefit, often diluting the movement's transformative goals. In the case of "wokeness," co-optation may involve the commercialization of social justice language, the tokenization of marginalized identities, or the depoliticization of the movement's demands.

One of the primary challenges of co-optation is the watering down of the radical and transformative nature of the Social Revolution. As the term "wokeness" becomes increasingly mainstream, its original meaning can be diluted or distorted to align with dominant narratives. This process can lead to the erasure of the movement's core demands and the co-optation of its symbols and language.

Commercial entities have also been known to co-opt "wokeness" to enhance their public image or marketability. In an era of conscious consumerism, some corporations may adopt social justice language without genuinely engaging in substantive actions to address systemic injustices. This commodification of "wokeness" can perpetuate a cycle of performative activism, where symbolic gestures are prioritized over meaningful change.

Another form of co-optation involves the tokenization of marginalized identities. In an attempt to appear inclusive, some institutions may showcase individuals from underrepresented communities without providing them with genuine decision-making power or addressing the systemic barriers they face. This tokenistic approach can undermine the movement's efforts to center marginalized voices and perspectives.

Co-optation can also manifest as the depoliticization of "wokeness," stripping the movement of its radical demands and reducing it to a superficial trend. The genuine pursuit of justice and equity may be replaced with surface-level discussions that fail to challenge the power structures perpetuating inequality.

To safeguard "wokeness" from co-optation, advocates must remain vigilant and strategic in their efforts. This includes actively challenging instances of co-optation within their communities and institutions, holding corporations accountable for their actions, and centering marginalized voices in decision-making processes.

Moreover, the Social Revolution must continuously redefine and reaffirm the meaning of "wokeness" in the context of its transformative goals. By emphasizing the interconnectedness of various forms of oppression and the collective responsibility to challenge systemic injustices, the movement can resist co-optation and remain true to its foundational principles.

The co-optation of "wokeness" poses significant challenges for the Social Revolution. As the movement gains visibility and influence, it becomes susceptible to being watered down, commodified, or tokenized by dominant forces. By recognizing and confronting co-optation, advocates can safeguard the integrity of the movement and drive meaningful progress toward a more just and equitable world. As we continue, we examine the strategies employed by activists to counter co-optation and preserve the authenticity of the Social Revolution.

### Navigating the Limits of "Wokeness"

As the Social Revolution gains momentum, it is essential to critically examine the limits of "wokeness" and its potential shortcomings. While "wokeness" has been instrumental in raising awareness and mobilizing collective action, it also faces challenges that require careful navigation. This section delves into the complexities of "wokeness," exploring its potential limitations and the strategies employed to ensure its transformative potential is fully realized.

One of the primary challenges of "wokeness" lies in its potential to become performative or superficial, as individuals and institutions adopt the language and symbols of social justice without making substantive contributions to systemic change. This performative aspect of "wokeness" can undermine the movement's authenticity and dilute its impact. As such, advocates must be vigilant in distinguishing genuine commitment to social justice from mere virtue signaling.

Another limitation of "wokeness" is the potential for it to be appropriated and co-opted by dominant institutions or political agendas. As the term gains popularity and recognition, there is a risk of it being distorted or commodified to align with mainstream narratives. This co-optation can lead to the depoliticization of "wokeness" and the erasure of its radical and transformative potential.

Furthermore, "wokeness" faces challenges in navigating the complexities of intersectionality and inclusivity. While it seeks to challenge multiple forms of oppression, it may not fully capture the diverse experiences and struggles faced by all marginalized communities. As advocates center their efforts on particular issues or identities, there is a risk of marginalizing others and perpetuating divisions within the movement.

In response to these limitations, activists must adopt a multifaceted approach to "wokeness" that centers authenticity, accountability, and intersectionality. Authenticity demands that individuals and institutions actively engage in self-reflection, continuously interrogating their motivations and actions to ensure they align with their professed commitment to justice and equity.

Accountability is crucial in holding individuals and institutions responsible for their actions and commitments. It requires transparency in advocacy efforts, a willingness to learn from mistakes, and a commitment to addressing the harm caused by performative or tokenistic actions.

Intersectionality serves as a guiding principle to ensure that "wokeness" is fully inclusive and considers the interlocking nature of oppression. By centering diverse voices and experiences, advocates can create a more nuanced and comprehensive understanding of social justice that addresses the complexities of intersecting identities.

To navigate the limits of "wokeness," the Social Revolution must remain grounded in its transformative vision. It must actively challenge co-optation, superficiality, and tokenism while fostering a culture of collective responsibility and accountability. By embracing the complexities of intersectionality and practicing authenticity in advocacy, the movement can overcome these challenges and fully realize the potential of "wokeness" as a driving force for social change.

"Wokeness" is a powerful concept that has ignited the Social Revolution and prompted widespread awareness of social injustices. However, it also faces challenges and limitations that demand critical reflection and strategic navigation. By centering authenticity, accountability, and intersectionality in the pursuit of justice and equity, advocates can maximize the impact of "wokeness" and create a more inclusive and transformative social revolution.

## The Power of Collective Storytelling

Storytelling emerges as a potent tool that transcends borders and builds bridges of understanding and empathy. Collective storytelling has the power to shape narratives, challenge dominant discourses, and foster a sense of interconnectedness among diverse communities. This section explores the transformative potential of collective storytelling in the Social Revolution and its role in empowering marginalized voices and mobilizing collective action.

Collective storytelling is rooted in the recognition that stories are not merely individual experiences but interconnected threads that weave together the fabric of society. By sharing their stories, individuals within the Social Revolution reclaim agency over their narratives, humanizing their struggles, and challenging dehumanizing stereotypes. This process of collective storytelling enables marginalized communities to shift the power dynamics of representation and dismantle the monolithic narratives perpetuated by dominant forces.

One of the key elements of collective storytelling is its ability to foster empathy and solidarity. Through listening to and engaging with diverse stories, individuals from different backgrounds can gain a deeper understanding of the systemic injustices faced by marginalized communities. Empathy serves as a catalyst for collective action, as individuals are inspired to stand in solidarity and advocate for change.

Moreover, collective storytelling serves as a powerful form of resistance against the erasure of history and culture. By passing down stories from one generation to another, communities preserve their heritage and resist efforts to suppress their voices. In this way, storytelling becomes an act of resilience and resistance, empowering communities to reclaim their identities and assert their rights.

The digital age has amplified the impact of collective storytelling, providing accessible platforms for individuals to share their stories with a global audience. Social media has become a conduit for narratives of resistance and resilience, enabling activists to bypass traditional gatekeepers and amplify marginalized voices. This democratization of storytelling has played a crucial role in catalyzing the Social Revolution, fostering a sense of interconnectedness among advocates worldwide.

Collective storytelling also challenges the dominant narratives propagated by oppressive systems. By dismantling monolithic and reductionist depictions of communities, it fosters a more nuanced understanding of the complexities of social injustices. This multidimensional portrayal serves as a counter-narrative that disrupts harmful stereotypes and challenges the status quo.

The power of collective storytelling in the Social Revolution is profound. Through sharing their stories, individuals within marginalized communities reclaim their agency, foster empathy, and resist erasure. This process of collective storytelling empowers communities to challenge dominant narratives and build bridges of solidarity. Going forward, we dig into the strategies employed by advocates to leverage the power of collective storytelling and amplify marginalized voices in the pursuit of justice and equity.

## Building Sustainable Social Movements

Building sustainable social movements is a critical aspect of the Social

Revolution, ensuring that the momentum for transformative change endures beyond momentary peaks of activism. Sustainability involves the creation of enduring structures, strategies, and networks that can weather challenges and continue the pursuit of justice and equity. This section explores the strategies employed by advocates to build sustainable social movements and foster lasting impact.

A key element in building sustainable social movements is the establishment of strong grassroots foundations. Grassroots movements emanate from the communities most affected by injustice, ensuring that advocacy efforts are rooted in the needs and aspirations of those directly impacted. This bottom-up approach fosters authentic and inclusive movements that are driven by the people they seek to serve.

Empowering local leadership is another crucial aspect of sustainability. By nurturing and supporting leaders within marginalized communities, social movements can sustain their impact and cultivate a new generation of advocates. This commitment to leadership development ensures that the movement's vision endures and remains relevant to the evolving needs of the community.

Strategic planning is essential in building sustainable social movements. Advocates must carefully consider their short-term and long-term goals, identifying achievable milestones while keeping their transformative vision in focus. This strategic approach enables movements to adapt to changing circumstances while staying true to their core values.

Building coalitions and alliances is a powerful strategy for sustainability. By forming partnerships with diverse organizations and communities, social movements can tap into a wider pool of resources, expertise, and support. These coalitions strengthen collective power, amplifying the movement's impact and creating a united front against systemic injustices.

Institutionalizing advocacy efforts is critical for sustainability. Social movements must work towards creating lasting change through policy reform, institutional accountability, and the incorporation of social justice principles into mainstream structures. Institutional change complements grassroots activism, creating lasting impact at a systemic level.

Engaging in sustained education and consciousness-raising is vital in building sustainable social movements. Advocates must continuously inform and educate the public about the issues at hand, challenging misinformation and fostering a more informed and engaged citizenry. Education empowers individuals to advocate for change and fosters a deeper commitment to social justice.

Recognizing the ebb and flow of momentum is essential for sustainability. Social movements may experience periods of heightened activism and periods of rest and reflection. Understanding that progress is often non-linear and requires resilience during challenging times is crucial in sustaining the movement's momentum.

Building sustainable social movements is fundamental to the longevity and impact of the Social Revolution. By adopting strategic planning, empowering local leadership, and forming alliances, advocates create enduring structures that can weather challenges and drive transformative change. Institutionalizing advocacy efforts and fostering consciousness-raising ensure that the movement's impact extends beyond fleeting moments of activism. As we move ahead, we'll take a more profound look into the strategies employed by advocates to build sustainable social movements and create lasting change in pursuit of a more just and equitable world.

## Beyond "Wokeness"
### Expanding the Frontiers of Activism

While "wokeness" has been a driving force in the Social Revolution, it is essential to recognize that the pursuit of justice and equity extends beyond mere awareness. This section explores the need to expand the frontiers of activism, going beyond "wokeness" to encompass substantive action, intersectional advocacy, and transformative change.

"Wokeness" has played a vital role in raising awareness of social injustices and challenging dominant narratives. However, awareness alone is not enough to drive meaningful change. Advocates must move beyond performative activism and embrace substantive action that addresses the root causes of inequality. This means engaging in concrete steps to dismantle oppressive systems and create lasting solutions.

Expanding the frontiers of activism requires a commitment to intersectionality, recognizing that social justice issues are interconnected and cannot be addressed in isolation. Advocates must center the voices and experiences of all marginalized communities, fostering a comprehensive understanding of the complex nature of oppression. By embracing intersectionality, the movement becomes more inclusive and capable of confronting the multiple layers of systemic injustice.

Transcending the limits of "wokeness" involves a deeper exploration of systemic change and transformative solutions. It requires reimagining societal structures and policies to create a more just and equitable world. Transformative change challenges the status quo, envisioning a society that prioritizes justice, equity, and liberation for all individuals.

Empowering grassroots movements and community-led initiatives is crucial in expanding the frontiers of activism. True transformative change often emerges from the collective efforts of those most affected by injustice. By supporting local leadership and amplifying community-driven solutions, advocates create a more sustainable and impactful movement.

Additionally, engaging in solidarity with global movements broadens the horizons of activism. The struggles for justice are not confined to national boundaries, and advocates must recognize the interconnectedness of social justice efforts worldwide. By building bridges with global allies, the movement becomes more powerful and better equipped to challenge systemic injustice on a global scale.

Ultimately, expanding the frontiers of activism means embodying the spirit of continuous learning and growth. Advocates must be willing to listen, learn, and evolve their strategies to remain relevant and effective in the pursuit of justice. The Social Revolution must be a living, breathing movement, responsive to the ever-changing landscape of social justice challenges.

While "wokeness" has been a catalyst for the Social Revolution, expanding the frontiers of activism demands substantive action, intersectional advocacy, and transformative change. By going beyond performative gestures and embracing grassroots initiatives, advocates can create a more inclusive, impactful, and sustainable movement. The pursuit of justice and equity requires a commitment to dismantling oppressive systems and centering the voices of all marginalized communities. As you continue reading, we introduce strategies employed by activists to expand the frontiers of activism and realize the transformative potential of the Social Revolution.

The Social Revolution is a dynamic and transformative movement driven by a commitment to justice, equity, and liberation. At its core, the Social Revolution seeks to challenge oppressive systems, amplify marginalized voices, and create a more just and equitable world. As we conclude, we reflect on the key themes explored throughout this chapter and underscore the importance of collective action, intersectionality, and sustainable activism in driving lasting change.

The enigma of "wokeness" has been instrumental in sparking awareness and mobilizing collective action. However, the transformation and expansion of "wokeness" have also exposed it to co-optation and challenges of performative activism. To harness the transformative power of "wokeness," advocates must navigate its complexities and uphold authenticity, accountability, and intersectionality in their advocacy efforts.

The rise of corporate co-optation poses a significant challenge to the Social Revolution. As the movement gains visibility and influence, there is a risk of its transformative goals being diluted or commodified for commercial gain. By actively challenging co-optation and fostering grassroots initiatives, advocates can preserve the integrity of the movement and remain true to its transformative vision.

The Social Revolution must go beyond mere awareness and embrace collective action. Building sustainable social movements involves strategic planning, empowering local leadership, and fostering coalitions to create enduring structures for transformative change. By engaging in sustained education and consciousness-raising, advocates can foster a more informed and engaged citizenry, driving meaningful progress over time.

The power of collective storytelling in the Social Revolution is profound. Through sharing diverse stories, individuals reclaim agency over their narratives, challenge dominant discourses, and foster empathy and solidarity. Collective storytelling becomes an act of resistance, empowering communities to resist erasure and reclaim their identities.

The Social Revolution must continuously strive to expand its frontiers, going beyond "wokeness" to address systemic change and intersectional advocacy. By centering the voices and experiences of all marginalized communities and engaging in transformative solutions, advocates can create a more inclusive, impactful, and enduring movement.

The Social Revolution is a journey of collective awakening, activism, and transformation. To realize its transformative potential, advocates must navigate the complexities of "wokeness," challenge co-optation, build sustainable movements, and go beyond performative gestures. By embracing intersectionality, collective storytelling, and sustainable activism, the Social Revolution can drive lasting change and pave the way towards a more just and equitable world. Up next, approaches employed by activists in their pursuit of justice and equity in a world fraught with challenges and opportunities for transformative change.

*"They turned 'woke' into a puppet, making it dance to the tune of ignorance."*

# CHAPTER 3
# THE RISE OF CORPORATE CO-OPTATION

The rise of corporate co-optation stands as a complex and multifaceted challenge. As the movement for justice and equity gains momentum, it also becomes a prime target for co-optation by powerful institutions seeking to capitalize on its popularity while diluting its transformative goals. This chapter delves into the phenomenon of corporate co-optation, exploring its origins, tactics, and implications for the Social Revolution.

At the heart of the Social Revolution lies a collective yearning for justice and a commitment to dismantling oppressive systems. Grassroots activists, advocates, and marginalized communities have long been at the forefront of driving transformative change. However, as the movement gains visibility and influence, corporations and dominant institutions are increasingly seeking to capitalize on its momentum.

Corporate co-optation involves the appropriation of social justice language, symbols, and causes by corporate entities for their benefit. In the pursuit of profit, some corporations adopt the appearance of social responsibility and activism without genuinely engaging in substantive action to address the root causes of injustice. By using the language of "wokeness" and social justice, these entities seek to enhance their public image and appeal to socially conscious consumers.

The motivations behind corporate co-optation can vary. Some corporations may be genuinely inspired by the principles of the Social Revolution and attempt to incorporate social justice into their business practices. However, this commitment often falls short, as it fails to address the systemic issues perpetuated by corporate structures.

On the other hand, some corporations may engage in performative activism, using social justice language as a marketing ploy to gain favor with consumers while remaining complicit in perpetuating oppressive systems. This form of co-optation undermines the authenticity of the movement and dilutes its transformative potential.

The consequences of corporate co-optation extend beyond mere marketing strategies. Co-optation can lead to the depoliticization and commodification of social justice causes, where advocacy becomes a marketable brand rather than a genuine commitment to change. In this context, the pursuit of justice is reduced to a superficial trend, disconnected from the collective struggle for liberation.

Furthermore, corporate co-optation can divert attention and resources away from grassroots initiatives and community-led movements. As corporations gain prominence and visibility in the social justice discourse, the voices of marginalized communities and the demands of transformative grassroots activism may be overshadowed or marginalized.

In this chapter, we go into the tactics employed by corporations to co-opt the Social Revolution, the implications of co-optation on the movement's integrity and effectiveness, and the strategies employed by advocates to challenge and resist corporate co-optation. By understanding the intricacies of this challenge, the movement can better protect its transformative goals and foster genuine change in pursuit of justice and equity.

## The "Wokeness" Trend in Marketing

The concept of "wokeness" has not only permeated activism and grassroots movements but also corporate marketing strategies. The "wokeness" trend in marketing refers to the deliberate adoption of social justice language and symbols by corporations to appeal to socially conscious consumers. As the pursuit of justice gains popularity and consumer sentiment shifts towards conscious consumption, corporations have recognized the potential profit in aligning themselves with social justice causes.

Consumers are increasingly seeking to support brands that appear to be socially responsible and aligned with their values. This shift in consumer behavior has led corporations to integrate "wokeness" into their marketing campaigns, hoping to attract a broader customer base and boost their bottom line.

One of the ways in which corporations co-opt the "wokeness" trend is through the use of inclusive and progressive messaging. Advertisements and branding materials feature diverse representation, socially conscious themes, and calls to action for positive change. Such messaging is carefully crafted to appeal to consumers who are committed to social justice causes, creating the perception that the brand aligns with their values.

The "wokeness" trend in marketing also involves corporate engagement with social justice issues. Companies may take public stances on hot-button topics, expressing solidarity with marginalized communities and advocating for change. While some corporations may genuinely care about these issues, others use them opportunistically as a marketing strategy, devoid of substantive action or systemic change.

The consequence of this trend is a phenomenon often referred to as "woke-washing" or "virtue signaling." Corporations may appear to be socially conscious and progressive, but their commitment to social justice often remains superficial and performative. This type of co-optation undermines the authenticity of the movement, reducing justice to a branding strategy rather than a transformative mission.

Moreover, the "wokeness" trend in marketing can create a sense of complacency among consumers. When corporations adopt the language of social justice, consumers may feel satisfied with their choices and perceive their support of these brands as a form of activism. However, this passive engagement may divert attention and resources away from genuine grassroots initiatives and transformative efforts.

The "wokeness" trend in marketing reflects the co-optation of social justice language and symbols by corporations for profit and public image enhancement. This form of co-optation can undermine the authenticity of the Social Revolution, diluting its transformative potential and diverting attention away from grassroots movements. As consumers, it is crucial to be discerning in our support of brands and demand genuine action and commitment to justice from corporations.

## "Woke" Corporate Campaigns: Genuine Allyship or Performative Gestures?

Corporations have increasingly sought to align themselves with social justice causes through "woke" corporate campaigns. These campaigns present corporations as allies and advocates for marginalized communities, but the authenticity of their commitment is often questioned. This section dives into the complexities of "woke" corporate campaigns, exploring whether they represent genuine allyship or mere performative gestures.

On the surface, "woke" corporate campaigns may seem like genuine displays of allyship and solidarity. These campaigns often feature diverse representation, socially conscious messaging, and endorsements of social justice causes. They may highlight donations to related charities or feature initiatives that purport to address systemic injustices.

However, the authenticity of these campaigns comes under scrutiny due to their limited scope and lack of substantive action. Critics argue that many "woke" corporate campaigns amount to performative gestures, where corporations seek to capitalize on social justice issues without making significant changes to their business practices or addressing the root causes of injustice.

Performative "woke-washing" can be harmful in several ways. First, it can divert attention and resources away from genuine grassroots movements and community-led initiatives. When corporations take center stage in social justice conversations, the voices of marginalized communities can be overshadowed, and their demands for systemic change may be ignored.

Second, performative "woke" campaigns risk trivializing the struggles of marginalized communities by reducing complex issues to catchy slogans and superficial messaging. This can perpetuate harmful stereotypes and erase the deeper and systemic issues that perpetuate inequality.

Furthermore, these campaigns can create a sense of complacency among consumers who may believe that supporting "woke" brands absolves them of the responsibility to actively engage in social justice efforts. Instead of driving substantive change, these campaigns may foster a sense of satisfaction based on symbolic gestures alone.

To distinguish genuine allyship from performative gestures, it is essential to assess the actions and long-term commitment of corporations. Genuine allyship goes beyond surface-level messaging and involves concrete actions that address systemic issues and dismantle oppressive structures.

Authentic "woke" corporate campaigns are backed by a commitment to diversity and inclusion within the company's workforce, leadership, and supply chains. They involve investing in community-led initiatives, supporting policy changes that promote justice, and addressing the impact of their business practices on marginalized communities.

The authenticity of "woke" corporate campaigns is a crucial aspect of the fight against co-optation in the Social Revolution. Advocates and consumers must critically evaluate the actions and commitments of corporations to discern between genuine allyship and performative gestures. To ensure that the movement remains true to its transformative goals, it is essential to resist "woke-washing" and demand substantive action and systemic change from corporations seeking to align themselves with social justice causes.

## The Capitalist Co-optation of "Wokeness"

As the Social Revolution gains momentum, the phenomenon of capitalist co-optation poses a significant threat to the authenticity and transformative potential of the movement. Capitalist co-optation refers to the integration of "wokeness" into the capitalist system, where social justice language and symbols are commodified and repurposed to serve capitalist interests. In this section, we explore the implications of capitalist co-optation on the Social Revolution and the ways in which it undermines the pursuit of justice and equity.

Profit maximization is the primary goal of corporations. As the "wokeness" trend gains traction and resonates with consumers, corporations recognize the potential financial gain in aligning their brand with social justice causes. Consequently, social justice language and symbols become marketing tools that can be manipulated to increase profits, often at the expense of authentic advocacy.

Capitalist co-optation of "wokeness" can lead to the watering down of the movement's transformative goals. As corporations seek to appeal to a broad customer base, they may avoid engaging with more radical and systemic demands put forth by grassroots activists. Instead, they opt for palatable and uncontroversial messaging that can be easily absorbed by mainstream consumers.

Moreover, capitalist co-optation can result in the erasure of the movement's radical origins. The Social Revolution emerged from the struggles and resistance of marginalized communities, seeking to dismantle oppressive systems and challenge the status quo. However, as corporations appropriate social justice language for their benefit, the radical roots of the movement can be obscured and diluted.

This co-optation also extends to the labor practices of corporations. While outwardly promoting "wokeness," some companies may exploit their workers, perpetuating oppressive labor conditions that directly contradict the values of justice and equity. This discrepancy between corporate branding and labor practices highlights the superficiality of capitalist co-optation.

Furthermore, capitalist co-optation commodifies social justice issues, turning them into marketable products. For example, during Pride Month, many corporations release rainbow-themed products and advertisements to capitalize on the LGBTQ+ rights movement. While some companies may donate a portion of profits to LGBTQ+ organizations, the commercialization of the movement can be seen as exploitative and trivializes the struggles of the LGBTQ+ community.

The capitalist co-optation of "wokeness" poses a significant challenge to the authenticity and transformative potential of the Social Revolution. By commodifying social justice language and symbols, corporations dilute the movement's radical goals and prioritize profit over meaningful change.

This co-optation erases the movement's grassroots origins and can perpetuate harmful labor practices. It also commodifies social justice issues, turning them into marketable products. As advocates, it is essential to resist capitalist co-optation and demand genuine commitment to justice and equity from corporations.

### The Whitewashing of "Wokeness"

The concept of "wokeness" has emerged as a powerful force for justice and equity. However, as corporations and dominant institutions seek to co-opt the movement, there is a troubling trend of whitewashing "wokeness." Whitewashing refers to the erasure or dilution of the racial dimensions of social justice causes, particularly in the context of corporate co-optation. In this section, we examine the implications of whitewashing on the Social Revolution and the ways in which it undermines the pursuit of racial justice.

The Social Revolution has been intrinsically linked to the struggles of marginalized communities, especially Black, Indigenous, and people of color (BIPOC) who have been disproportionately affected by systemic injustice. "Wokeness" originated from these communities' collective resistance against oppression and has been a vehicle for their demands for justice and equality.

However, as corporations seek to align themselves with the movement, there is a danger of whitewashing the narrative. Some corporations may adopt social justice language and symbols while erasing the racial dimensions of the issues at hand. This erasure can perpetuate the myth of a colorblind society, obscuring the systemic racism that underlies social disparities and injustices.

Whitewashing "wokeness" can also lead to the marginalization of BIPOC activists and advocates. As corporations co-opt the language of the movement, they may prioritize the voices of white influencers and celebrities over BIPOC activists who have long been at the forefront of the struggle for justice. This not only erases the contributions of BIPOC activists but also perpetuates the imbalance of power within the movement.

Moreover, the whitewashing of "wokeness" can result in performative gestures that do little to address the root causes of racial injustice. Corporations may release statements and campaigns that appear to be in support of racial justice causes, but without substantive action and investment in BIPOC communities, these efforts remain superficial.

The consequences of whitewashing "wokeness" are profound. It perpetuates the narrative that social justice issues are universal and colorblind, erasing the unique struggles faced by BIPOC communities. It also allows corporations to co-opt the language of the movement without taking meaningful steps towards racial equity.

The whitewashing of "wokeness" presents a significant challenge to the Social Revolution's pursuit of racial justice and equity. By erasing the racial dimensions of social justice causes, corporations and dominant institutions can co-opt the movement without addressing the root causes of racial injustice. As advocates, it is crucial to challenge whitewashing and demand genuine commitment to racial justice from those seeking to align themselves with the movement. Next, we will explore strategies to resist whitewashing and center the voices and experiences of BIPOC communities in the pursuit of justice and equity.

## Backlash and Public Perception

As corporations increasingly co-opt the language of "wokeness" for their benefit, a growing backlash has emerged from both activists and the public. The rise of corporate co-optation has raised questions about the authenticity of these efforts and the impact on the Social Revolution's credibility. In this section, we explore the backlash against corporate co-optation and its implications for public perception of the movement.

One of the primary concerns raised by the backlash is the superficiality of corporate co-optation. Critics argue that many "woke" corporate campaigns and initiatives are merely performative gestures, lacking substantive action to address systemic issues. As consumers become more discerning and aware of these tactics, they may question the authenticity of corporate efforts and feel disillusioned by companies that engage in "wokeness" without real commitment.

Moreover, the backlash highlights the risk of "woke-washing" leading to consumer cynicism. When corporations exploit social justice language for profit, it can erode public trust and dampen enthusiasm for the Social Revolution. The movement's transformative goals may be undermined by the perception that corporations are merely capitalizing on a trend, rather than genuinely advocating for change.

The backlash against corporate co-optation can also lead to a reevaluation of corporate responsibility and ethical consumerism. As consumers become more conscious of the impact of their choices, they may actively seek to support brands that demonstrate genuine commitment to social justice causes. This shift in consumer behavior can challenge corporations to be more transparent and accountable in their advocacy efforts.

Furthermore, the backlash extends to the movement's credibility as a whole. The co-optation of "wokeness" by corporations can create confusion about the movement's goals and dilute its transformative vision. Activists may worry that their work is being co-opted and that the movement's radical demands for change are being co-opted into a commercialized and commodified message.

While the backlash against corporate co-optation is essential for maintaining the integrity of the Social Revolution, it also raises questions about the sustainability of the movement. To effectively challenge oppressive systems, advocates must remain vigilant against co-optation while also driving meaningful change. This requires a delicate balance of holding corporations accountable while fostering genuine alliances with those willing to engage in substantive action.

The backlash against corporate co-optation underscores the importance of authentic advocacy and the impact of performative gestures on public perception. As the movement for justice and equity gains visibility, it must navigate the complexities of co-optation while maintaining its transformative goals. By challenging corporate "woke-washing" and demanding substantive action, the Social Revolution can preserve its credibility and continue to drive meaningful change. Follow us as we explore strategies to resist and challenge corporate co-optation, fostering a more accountable and genuine commitment to justice and equity.

## Impacts on the "Wokeness" Movement

The co-optation of "wokeness" by corporations has significant impacts on the broader movement for justice and equity. As social justice language and symbols are appropriated for profit, the "wokeness" movement faces both challenges and opportunities in its pursuit of transformative change. In this section, we explore the impacts of corporate co-optation on the "wokeness" movement and how advocates can respond to preserve its integrity.

One of the immediate impacts of corporate co-optation is the potential dilution of the movement's radical goals. As corporations adopt social justice language for marketing purposes, the transformative demands of the movement may be watered down to appeal to a broader audience. This can lead to a loss of focus on systemic change and perpetuate a superficial understanding of justice and equity.

Moreover, the co-optation of "wokeness" can overshadow the voices of grassroots activists and community-led initiatives. As corporations gain visibility and prominence in social justice conversations, the struggles and demands of marginalized communities may be sidelined or overlooked. This imbalance of power can undermine the movement's ability to drive substantive change.

Additionally, corporate co-optation can lead to a shift in public perception of the "wokeness" movement. As consumers become more aware of performative gestures and superficial engagement, they may view the movement with skepticism and mistrust. This can dampen enthusiasm and support for social justice causes, making it challenging to mobilize public support for meaningful change.

However, the impacts of corporate co-optation also present opportunities for advocates to respond strategically. By raising awareness about the dangers of "woke-washing" and challenging corporations to back their messaging with substantive action, advocates can hold corporations accountable for their co-optation tactics.

Furthermore, the co-optation of "wokeness" by corporations highlights the need for intersectional and community-led approaches to justice and equity. Marginalized communities must remain central to the movement's leadership and decision-making processes, ensuring that their struggles and demands are at the forefront of advocacy efforts.

The impacts of corporate co-optation also underscore the importance of collective action and solidarity. By fostering alliances with organizations and individuals committed to transformative change, the "wokeness" movement can resist co-optation and maintain its focus on dismantling oppressive systems.

The co-optation of "wokeness" by corporations has far-reaching impacts on the broader movement for justice and equity. While corporate co-optation poses challenges to the movement's authenticity and transformative goals, it also provides opportunities for advocates to respond strategically and center the voices of marginalized communities. By resisting "woke-washing," promoting intersectionality, and fostering collective action, the "wokeness" movement can navigate the complexities of corporate co-optation and continue to drive meaningful change.

### Toward Authentic Corporate Social Responsibility

While corporate co-optation poses challenges to the authenticity of the "wokeness" movement, it also presents an opportunity for corporations to embrace genuine corporate social responsibility (CSR). Authentic CSR involves a commitment to social justice causes that extends beyond superficial gestures and marketing strategies. In this section, we explore the path toward authentic CSR and its potential to drive meaningful change in the pursuit of justice and equity.

One of the key elements of authentic CSR is transparency and accountability. Corporations must be open and honest about their commitment to social justice causes, and their actions should align with their stated values. This includes disclosing information about their supply chain practices, diversity and inclusion initiatives, and efforts to address systemic issues within their industry.

Moreover, authentic CSR requires long-term engagement with social justice causes. Rather than engaging in short-term, reactive campaigns, corporations should adopt a sustained commitment to addressing the root causes of injustice. This may involve supporting community-led initiatives, investing in education and advocacy efforts, and actively working to dismantle oppressive systems within their own organizations.

Authentic CSR also necessitates a willingness to listen to and collaborate with grassroots activists and marginalized communities. Rather than co-opting the language of the "wokeness" movement, corporations should actively seek input from those most affected by systemic injustices. This includes creating spaces for dialogue, providing resources and support to community-led initiatives, and leveraging their platforms to amplify marginalized voices.

Additionally, authentic CSR involves a recognition of the limitations of corporate power. While corporations can play a role in driving change, they cannot replace the collective power of grassroots activism and community-led movements. Instead of attempting to lead the movement, corporations should use their resources and influence to support and uplift existing efforts for justice.

By embracing authentic CSR, corporations have the potential to be powerful allies in the fight for justice and equity. When they commit to systemic change, dismantle oppressive practices, and actively engage with social justice causes, they can make a meaningful impact on the movement's goals.

The rise of corporate co-optation poses challenges to the authenticity of the "wokeness" movement. However, it also presents an opportunity for corporations to embrace authentic CSR and drive meaningful change. By being transparent, accountable, and committed to long-term engagement with social justice causes, corporations can play a supportive role in the pursuit of justice and equity. Collaborating with grassroots activists and recognizing the limits of their power, corporations can be genuine allies in the Social Revolution.

## Reclaiming "Wokeness" from Corporate Clutches

As corporate co-optation of "wokeness" becomes more prevalent, advocates and activists must work to reclaim the integrity of the movement from corporate clutches. Reclaiming "wokeness" involves asserting the grassroots origins of the Social Revolution and challenging the superficiality of corporate engagement with social justice causes. In this section, we explore strategies to resist corporate co-optation and reclaim the transformative power of "wokeness."

One of the essential strategies in reclaiming "wokeness" is education and awareness-raising. Advocates must actively expose and challenge "woke-washing" tactics employed by corporations, educating the public about the dangers of performative gestures and superficial engagement. By increasing awareness, consumers can make more informed choices and demand authentic action from corporations.

Central to the process of reclaiming "wokeness" is elevating the voices and experiences of marginalized communities. Grassroots activists and community-led initiatives must remain at the forefront of the movement, shaping its agenda and goals. Corporations seeking to engage in social justice causes must listen to these voices and center their perspectives in their efforts.

Moreover, advocates can actively challenge corporations that engage in "wokeness" without genuine commitment. This can be achieved through public pressure, social media campaigns, and collective action to hold corporations accountable for their actions. By amplifying authentic voices and demanding substantive change, advocates can resist the co-optation of "wokeness."

Collaboration and alliances between grassroots activists and corporate entities can also play a role in reclaiming "wokeness." However, these partnerships must be grounded in mutual respect and a commitment to transformative change. Corporations should support grassroots initiatives through financial and logistical resources, while activists can provide valuable insights and perspectives on social justice causes.

Furthermore, reclaiming "wokeness" involves envisioning and promoting alternative models of business and economic systems. Socially responsible businesses that prioritize equity, diversity, and sustainable practices can serve as examples of authentic corporate social responsibility. By promoting and supporting these alternative models, advocates can challenge the prevailing capitalist co-optation of "wokeness."

Reclaiming "wokeness" from corporate clutches is essential for preserving the integrity and transformative potential of the Social Revolution. By increasing awareness, centering the voices of marginalized communities, holding corporations accountable, and fostering authentic collaborations, advocates can resist co-optation and drive meaningful change. Reclaiming "wokeness" is not just about resisting corporate co-optation but also about imagining and building a more just and equitable future.

## An Intersectional Approach to Corporate Accountability

Addressing corporate co-optation of "wokeness" requires an intersectional approach to corporate accountability. An intersectional approach recognizes that social injustices are interconnected and overlapping, affecting individuals differently based on their intersecting identities and experiences. By applying this lens to corporate accountability, advocates can challenge co-optation more effectively and center the experiences of marginalized communities. In this section, we explore the importance of an intersectional approach to corporate accountability and its potential to foster genuine change.

An intersectional approach to corporate accountability involves recognizing the ways in which different forms of oppression intersect and reinforce each other. For example, the experiences of a Black woman may be distinct from those of a white woman or a Black man, as they face unique and compounded forms of discrimination. Corporations must consider these intersecting identities when engaging in social justice causes to avoid perpetuating one-dimensional narratives.

Moreover, an intersectional approach challenges corporations to address systemic issues rather than merely addressing surface-level symptoms. For example, a corporation that releases a diversity and inclusion statement without addressing racial pay disparities within its workforce may be engaging in performative gestures rather than genuine commitment to justice. An intersectional analysis requires a more comprehensive examination of corporate practices and their impacts on marginalized communities.

An essential aspect of an intersectional approach is involving diverse voices in decision-making processes. Corporations must actively seek input and feedback from employees and stakeholders with diverse perspectives and experiences. By fostering inclusive spaces, corporations can avoid tokenistic engagement and ensure that marginalized communities are not merely represented but actively empowered.

An intersectional approach also calls for corporate entities to confront their own complicity in systemic oppression. This may involve examining supply chains for exploitative practices, acknowledging historical ties to oppression, and making amends for past harms. Holding themselves accountable and taking concrete steps toward rectification is crucial for meaningful engagement with social justice causes.

Furthermore, corporations can adopt an intersectional lens in their philanthropic efforts. Rather than engaging in one-off donations or charity work, they can invest in organizations and initiatives led by marginalized communities, amplifying their impact and leadership. By supporting long-term community-led efforts, corporations can foster authentic change and address the root causes of injustice.

An intersectional approach to corporate accountability is crucial for resisting co-optation and fostering genuine change within the "wokeness" movement. By recognizing the interconnectedness of social injustices, involving diverse voices, confronting complicity, and supporting community-led initiatives, corporations can move beyond performative gestures and authentically engage with social justice causes. This approach empowers advocates to challenge corporate co-optation effectively and center the experiences of marginalized communities in the pursuit of justice and equity. In the subsequent sections, we will explore additional strategies to challenge and resist corporate co-optation, ensuring that the Social Revolution remains true to its transformative vision.

The rise of corporate co-optation poses significant challenges to the authenticity and integrity of the "wokeness" movement. As corporations seek to profit from social justice language and symbols, they risk diluting the transformative goals of the Social Revolution and undermining the collective efforts of grassroots activists. However, this chapter has also illuminated opportunities for advocates to resist and challenge corporate co-optation while centering the voices and experiences of marginalized communities.

Throughout this chapter, we explored the various ways in which corporations engage in "woke-washing" and superficial engagement with social justice causes. We analyzed the impact of co-optation on the movement's credibility, public perception, and the voices of marginalized communities. We also examined the potential for corporations to embrace authentic corporate social responsibility (CSR) and contribute meaningfully to the pursuit of justice and equity.

Key strategies to combat corporate co-optation include education and awareness-raising to expose performative gestures, holding corporations accountable through public pressure and collective action, and fostering alliances with socially responsible businesses and community-led initiatives. Moreover, an intersectional approach to corporate accountability has emerged as a powerful means of resisting co-optation and ensuring that social justice causes remain at the forefront of advocacy efforts.

As the "wokeness" movement continues to gain visibility and momentum, the challenges of corporate co-optation will persist. However, advocates can draw inspiration from the resilience and determination of grassroots activists who have long been at the forefront of the struggle for justice and equity. By reclaiming "wokeness" from corporate clutches, embracing an intersectional approach to accountability, and challenging co-optation at every turn, the Social Revolution can remain a transformative force for meaningful change.

To preserve the authenticity of the "wokeness" movement, it is crucial for advocates to resist superficial gestures and demand substantive action from corporations. By centering the voices and experiences of marginalized communities and fostering genuine collaboration and partnerships, the Social Revolution can build a more inclusive and equitable future.

Corporate co-optation is not an insurmountable obstacle but rather an opportunity for advocates to assert the transformative vision of the "wokeness" movement. By continuing to challenge co-optation, centering marginalized voices, and adopting an intersectional approach to accountability, advocates can foster authentic change and drive the pursuit of justice and equity.

*"They took the word 'woke' and turned it into a weapon of mass deception."*

## CHAPTER 4
# THE WOKE INDUSTRIAL COMPLEX

The term "woke" originally emerged from AAVE as a call to heightened awareness of social and political issues, particularly regarding systemic racism and social injustice. Over time, "woke" has evolved into a broader concept, encompassing a commitment to challenging oppressive structures and promoting social consciousness. However, as the Social Revolution gained momentum, the term has been co-opted by various actors, including corporations, media outlets, and political entities. This co-optation has given rise to what can be described as the "Woke Industrial Complex."

The "Woke Industrial Complex" refers to a network of powerful interests, both corporate and political, that exploit "wokeness" for their gain. This chapter delves into the complexities of the Woke Industrial Complex and its implications for the "wokeness" movement. We will examine how corporations, politicians, and media outlets have harnessed the language of "wokeness" for profit and influence, while also addressing the tensions and controversies that arise within the movement itself.

The Woke Industrial Complex has been fueled by the commercial-ization of social justice causes. As the demand for "wokeness" grows among consumers, corporations have sought to capitalize on this trend. They use social justice messaging in advertising, branding, and marketing campaigns, aiming to appeal to socially conscious con-sumers. While some corporations genuinely engage with social justice issues, others use "wokeness" as a marketing strategy without address-ing systemic injustices within their own operations.

Similarly, political actors have recognized the potential of "wokeness" to mobilize voters and gain support. They deploy social justice rhe-tric to appeal to progressive constituencies while avoiding substantive policy changes. This political co-optation has sparked debates within the movement about the dangers of being reduced to a mere buzz-word rather than a vehicle for transformative change.

The media's role in the Woke Industrial Complex is also critical. As the public's attention shifts toward social justice issues, media outlets often amplify certain voices and narratives while marginalizing others. This selective framing can impact the movement's visibility and the diversity of perspectives represented. Additionally, media sensationalism and performative gestures can detract from substantive discussions about systemic change.

The Woke Industrial Complex presents both opportunities and chal-lenges for the "wokeness" movement. While heightened awareness of social issues is essential, the co-optation of "wokeness" by powerful actors raises questions about authenticity and genuine commitment to social justice. As the movement navigates this complex landscape, ad-vocates must remain vigilant and strategic in challenging co-optation, while preserving the transformative vision of the Social Revolution.

## The Profit Motive: Capitalizing on "Wokeness"

Across the malleable landscape of social consciousness, the concept of "wokeness" has become a powerful force for change. However, the commercialization of social justice causes has given rise to the Profit Motive within the Woke Industrial Complex. Corporations have recognized the potential of "wokeness" as a marketable commodity, and this section explores how they capitalize on the movement for their financial gain, while also addressing the ethical implications of this commodification.

One of the primary ways in which corporations capitalize on "wokeness" is through performative activism. This involves the public display of support for social justice causes without substantive action or investment in change. Corporations may release statements, change their logos temporarily, or engage in one-off donations to capitalize on trending social justice issues without committing to meaningful systemic change. This type of "wokeness" marketing is often criticized for being superficial and lacking authenticity.

Moreover, the profit motive can lead to the co-optation of grassroots activism. When corporations adopt social justice language and symbols for marketing purposes, they risk overshadowing the voices and efforts of community-led initiatives. By presenting themselves as champions of "wokeness," corporations may divert attention and resources away from genuine grassroots movements working toward transformative change.

Furthermore, the commodification of "wokeness" can result in the watering down of social justice messaging. In an attempt to appeal to a broader audience, corporations may dilute the radical goals of the "wokeness" movement. This dilution can lead to a superficial understanding of social justice, focusing on individual actions and personal choices rather than systemic transformation.

Additionally, the profit motive can lead to the exploitation of marginalized identities and experiences. Some corporations engage within "wokeness" marketing that appropriates cultural symbols or appropriates the struggles of marginalized communities for profit. This appropriation can perpetuate harmful stereotypes and trivialize the lived experiences of those affected by systemic oppression.

While the profit motive within the Woke Industrial Complex may bring short-term gains for corporations, it also raises ethical concerns and can undermine the authenticity of the "wokeness" movement. Advocates and consumers alike must remain critical and discerning, demanding genuine commitment to social justice causes from corporations rather than superficial gestures.

The Profit Motive within the Woke Industrial Complex represents a significant challenge to the authenticity and integrity of the "wokeness" movement. While corporations may seek to capitalize on social justice causes for financial gain, this commodification risks diluting the movement's transformative potential. As advocates navigate this landscape, they must be vigilant in challenging performative activism and demanding substantive action and accountability from corporations.

## Media, Branding, and "Wokeness"

The role of the media in shaping public perception and discourse cannot be overstated. Within the Woke Industrial Complex, media outlets play a critical role in amplifying "wokeness" messaging and influencing public sentiment. This section explores the dynamic relationship between media, branding, and "wokeness," examining how the media's portrayal of social justice issues can impact the movement's visibility, authenticity, and transformative potential.

Media outlets have the power to shape narratives and frame social justice issues in ways that influence public opinion. They can either be allies in elevating the voices of marginalized communities and challenging systemic injustice or contribute to the commercialization and dilution of "wokeness" for profit. The selective coverage and sensationalism of social justice topics can impact the public's understanding of complex issues, shaping perceptions of the movement and its goals.

Within the Woke Industrial Complex, branding plays a significant role in shaping corporate identity and consumer perception. Corporations often use "wokeness" branding to align themselves with social justice values and appeal to socially conscious consumers. This branding strategy may involve the use of diverse models, social justice slogans, and imagery associated with social movements. However, the genuineness of such branding efforts is often questioned, with critics pointing out the dissonance between corporate actions and the values they claim to uphold.

Furthermore, the media's portrayal of "wokeness" can impact the diversity of voices represented within the movement. Media outlets may prioritize certain perspectives, often those of celebrities or influential figures, while marginalizing grassroots activists and community leaders. This selective framing can distort the public's understanding of the movement's goals and the diversity of experiences that inform its advocacy.

Additionally, media outlets may engage in "wokeness" as a performative gesture to appeal to their audience or maintain relevance. This form of performative media activism can be harmful as it detracts from substantive reporting on social justice issues and undermines the integrity of the movement. Sensationalism and clickbait tactics can overshadow genuine reporting on systemic injustices and transformative efforts.

The relationship between media, branding, and "wokeness" is complex and multifaceted within the Woke Industrial Complex. The media's role in shaping narratives and framing social justice issues can impact the movement's visibility and authenticity. Corporations' use of "wokeness" branding raises questions about the genuineness of their commitment to social justice causes. As advocates navigate this terrain, they must critically assess media portrayals of "wokeness" and demand that corporations demonstrate substantive action rather than performative gestures.

### The Role of Celebrity and Influencers

Within the Woke Industrial Complex, the influence of celebrities and social media influencers cannot be underestimated. These high-profile figures have enormous platforms and followings, making them powerful agents in shaping public opinion and discourse around social justice issues. However, their involvement in the "wokeness" movement raises questions about authenticity, accountability, and the potential for performative activism.

Celebrities and influencers often use their platforms to advocate for social justice causes, drawing attention to systemic injustices and marginalized communities. Their engagement can bring much-needed visibility to important issues and mobilize their fan base for positive change. However, their role also presents challenges, particularly when their advocacy is not matched with substantive action.

The concept of "celebrity activism" has been subject to scrutiny, as some celebrities engage in superficial gestures without a deeper commitment to social justice causes. Their involvement in the "wokeness" movement can sometimes be seen as performative, with actions that are more about enhancing their public image rather than driving transformative change.

Moreover, the influence of celebrities and influencers can overshadow the work of grassroots activists and community-led initiatives. Media attention often gravitates toward high-profile figures, while the voices and experiences of those on the ground are marginalized. This can lead to a distortion of the movement's goals and a lack of understanding of the broader systemic issues at hand.

However, there are instances where celebrities and influencers have effectively used their platforms to advance social justice causes. When aligned with grassroots efforts and genuine commitment, their influence can drive tangible change and elevate underrepresented voices. Their involvement can also inspire their followers to engage with social justice issues, sparking conversations and action.

To address the potential pitfalls of celebrity involvement, accountability is essential. Advocates must hold celebrities and influencers accountable for their actions and demand transparency in their advocacy efforts. This may involve scrutinizing their endorsements, partnerships, and financial contributions to ensure they align with their stated values.

The role of celebrities and influencers in the Woke Industrial Complex is both influential and complex. Their engagement can bring much-needed attention to social justice causes, but it also raises questions about authenticity and accountability. As advocates navigate this landscape, they must critically assess the impact of celebrity activism and strive to center the voices and experiences of grassroots activists. By demanding accountability and fostering genuine collaborations, the "wokeness" movement can harness the influence of celebrities and influencers for meaningful change.

## Tokenism and Diversity Theater

Tokenism and diversity theater are pervasive issues within the Woke Industrial Complex, particularly in corporate settings and media representation. These practices involve superficial gestures aimed at appearing inclusive and diverse without addressing the root causes of systemic inequities. This section explores how tokenism and diversity theater undermine the authenticity and transformative potential of the "wokeness" movement.

Tokenism occurs when individuals from underrepresented groups are included merely as symbolic gestures, without genuine empowerment or meaningful involvement. In corporate settings, this may manifest as hiring a few people from marginalized backgrounds to create the appearance of diversity without addressing discriminatory practices or promoting inclusion. Tokenism fosters a culture where those from underrepresented groups may feel isolated and undervalued, perpetuating systemic inequalities.

Similarly, diversity theater refers to the performative display of diversity without a commitment to systemic change. Corporations and media outlets may engage in diversity theater by showcasing diverse faces or perspectives in marketing materials, advertisements, or TV shows, but neglect to address the systemic barriers that prevent meaningful representation and inclusion.

Both tokenism and diversity theater can lead to the commodification of diversity, reducing marginalized identities to mere checkboxes for corporate or media branding. This shallow approach fails to recognize the complexities and lived experiences of underrepresented communities, reinforcing harmful stereotypes and undermining the potential for authentic engagement with social justice causes.

Moreover, tokenism and diversity theater can create a false sense of progress, allowing corporations and media outlets to claim they are addressing issues of diversity and inclusion without enacting substantive change. This diversionary tactic can undermine genuine efforts to challenge systemic oppression and can be perceived as disingenuous by the public.

To combat tokenism and diversity theater, advocates must demand meaningful representation and inclusion. This involves holding corporations and media outlets accountable for their practices and advocating for concrete steps to promote diversity and address systemic inequities. Genuine inclusion requires a commitment to dismantling discriminatory practices and centering the voices of marginalized communities.

Tokenism and diversity theater are harmful practices within the Woke Industrial Complex that undermine the transformative potential of the "wokeness" movement. By demanding genuine representation and inclusion, advocates can challenge corporations and media outlets to go beyond performative gestures and enact substantive change. Addressing tokenism and diversity theater is essential for fostering an authentic and inclusive "wokeness" movement that truly challenges systemic injustice.

## The Co-optation of Social Movements

The co-optation of social movements is a common phenomenon within the Woke Industrial Complex. Co-optation occurs when powerful actors, such as corporations or politicians, adopt the language and symbols of social justice causes to advance their own interests, often diluting or distorting the original goals of the movement. This section examines how co-optation can undermine the authenticity and effectiveness of social justice advocacy.

When corporations engage in "wokeness" marketing or adopt social justice messaging, they risk appropriating the struggles of marginalized communities for profit. The co-optation of social justice language allows corporations to present themselves as allies without addressing the root causes of systemic injustice. This can create a false sense of progress and divert attention from the urgent need for substantive change.

Politicians may also engage in co-optation by employing social justice rhetoric to gain support from progressive constituencies. However, if their actions do not align with their words, this can lead to disillusionment and a lack of trust in the political system. Co-optation in politics can also lead to the watering down of social justice causes, as politicians may prioritize popular appeal over genuine transformative policies.

Furthermore, the co-optation of social movements can lead to tensions within the movement itself. Grassroots activists may feel marginalized or silenced as powerful actors dominate the narrative and resources. This can result in internal divisions and a dilution of the movement's goals and messaging.

Moreover, the co-optation of social justice causes can create a false sense of accomplishment, as performative gestures and superficial engagement can be mistaken for substantive change. This can hinder genuine efforts to challenge systemic injustices and erode the transformative potential of the "wokeness" movement.

To address the co-optation of social movements, advocates must remain vigilant and critical. They should demand transparency and accountability from corporations and politicians, ensuring that their actions align with their stated commitment to social justice. Grassroots activists must also continue to center their voices and experiences within the movement, resisting the marginalization that can arise from co-optation.

The co-optation of social movements is a significant challenge within the Woke Industrial Complex. When corporations and politicians appropriate the language and symbols of social justice for their gain, they risk undermining the authenticity and transformative potential of the "wokeness" movement. Advocates must remain vigilant in challenging co-optation and demanding genuine commitment to social justice causes from powerful actors. By centering the voices of grassroots activists and promoting substantive change, the "wokeness" movement can retain its integrity and drive meaningful progress.

### Activism as Branding: "Brandvocacy"

"Brandvocacy" refers to the practice of corporations engaging in activism or social justice causes as a branding strategy. In the Woke Industrial Complex, some corporations adopt social justice issues as part of their brand identity to appeal to socially conscious consumers. While this form of "wokeness" marketing can raise awareness about important issues, it also raises concerns about authenticity and the potential for performative gestures.

"Brandvocacy" involves corporations aligning themselves with specific social justice causes to create a positive brand image and gain consumer loyalty. They may sponsor events, donate to related charities, or engage in public statements to signal their support for social justice issues. While some corporations may genuinely invest in social justice causes, others may use "brandvocacy" as a veneer to improve their public image without substantive systemic change.

This form of "wokeness" marketing can blur the line between genuine advocacy and commercial interests. The use of social justice causes as branding tools risks reducing important issues to mere marketing strategies, thereby trivializing the experiences of those affected by systemic injustice.

Moreover, "brandvocacy" can contribute to the erasure of the radical roots of social justice movements. By co-opting social justice language for branding purposes, corporations may dilute the transformative goals of the "wokeness" movement. This can create a disconnect between the genuine advocacy of grassroots activists and the superficial gestures of corporate "brandvocates."

Critics argue that "brandvocacy" can lead to a performative approach to social justice, with corporations engaging in superficial gestures that lack meaningful impact. This can perpetuate a sense of complacency among consumers who may mistake symbolic gestures for substantive change.

To address "brandvocacy" within the Woke Industrial Complex, advocates must demand genuine commitment to social justice causes from corporations. This involves holding corporations accountable for their actions and advocating for substantive change that addresses systemic inequities. Transparency is crucial, and consumers should critically assess the authenticity of a corporation's engagement with social justice issues.

"Brandvocacy" is a prevalent phenomenon within the Woke Industrial Complex, where corporations engage in activism as a branding strategy. While some corporations may genuinely invest in social justice causes, "brandvocacy" raises concerns about authenticity and performative gestures. Advocates must remain critical and hold corporations accountable for their actions, demanding genuine commitment to social justice causes. By challenging the commodification of social justice, the "wokeness" movement can maintain its transformative potential.

## Resistance and Critiques

As the Woke Industrial Complex continues to shape the landscape of social justice advocacy, it is met with both resistance and critiques from various quarters. While the movement has brought important issues to the forefront and inspired meaningful change, it has also faced challenges and scrutiny. This section examines the different forms of resistance and critiques faced by the "wokeness" movement.

One of the primary critiques of the Woke Industrial Complex comes from those who argue that the movement focuses too heavily on individual actions and performative gestures rather than systemic change. Critics argue that the commercialization of social justice issues and the rise of "wokeness" marketing within corporations can divert attention and resources away from addressing the root causes of systemic oppression.

Another critique centers around the potential for "wokeness" to be co-opted and diluted, leading to the whitewashing of social justice causes and the erasure of marginalized voices. Some critics argue that corporations and powerful actors may engage in "wokeness" marketing as a way to appear progressive without enacting substantive change.

Additionally, there are concerns about the impact of cancel culture within the "wokeness" movement. While calling out harmful behavior and holding individuals accountable can be important, the excessive use of cancel culture can stifle constructive dialogue and impede opportunities for growth and learning.

Moreover, the increasing emphasis on "virtue signaling" or the performative display of social justice values on social media has been criticized for lacking genuine commitment to change. This form of activism can sometimes be more focused on appearing "woke" rather than driving substantive transformation.

Despite these critiques, the "wokeness" movement has also faced resistance from conservative voices who seek to delegitimize the pursuit of social justice and equality. These critics may label the movement as divisive or dismiss it as political correctness, often seeking to undermine its goals and impact.

In response to both internal and external critiques, advocates within the "wokeness" movement are engaging in ongoing discussions about the most effective strategies for transformative change. This includes a renewed focus on systemic issues, promoting genuine allyship, and encouraging open dialogue and learning.

The Woke Industrial Complex faces both resistance and critiques from various angles. While there are valid concerns about the co-optation and commodification of social justice, the movement has also brought important issues to the forefront and inspired meaningful change. By addressing internal critiques and engaging in constructive dialogue, the "wokeness" movement can navigate these challenges and continue its pursuit of justice and equality.

## The Impact on Social Justice Discourse

The rise of the Woke Industrial Complex has had a profound impact on social justice discourse, shaping the ways in which issues of equity, diversity, and inclusion are discussed and understood. While the movement has brought important social justice issues to the forefront, it has also sparked debates about language, tactics, and the effectiveness of advocacy. This section explores the impact of the Woke Industrial Complex on social justice discourse.

One significant impact of the Woke Industrial Complex is the increased visibility of social justice issues in public discourse. The movement has brought attention to systemic inequities and injustices faced by marginalized communities, challenging the dominant narrative and demanding a more inclusive society.

Moreover, the use of social media and digital platforms has amplified the voices of grassroots activists and empowered individuals to engage in social justice discourse. Hashtags, viral campaigns, and online organizing have facilitated collective action and mobilization, allowing for greater public participation in social justice advocacy.

However, the Woke Industrial Complex has also prompted debates about the language and terminology used in social justice discourse. The coining and appropriation of terms like "wokeness" have sparked discussions about the efficacy and potential misinterpretation of social justice language, especially when used in corporate or performative contexts.

Additionally, the movement's emphasis on calling out harmful behaviors and holding individuals accountable has led to discussions about the impact of cancel culture on public discourse. While some argue that cancel culture can be a necessary tool for accountability, others worry that it can inhibit open dialogue and limit opportunities for growth and education.

Moreover, the commodification and commercialization of social justice issues by corporations have led to debates about the sincerity of "wokeness" marketing. Critics argue that corporate engagement in social justice causes can dilute the transformative potential of the movement, while advocates call for genuine action and systemic change.

The impact of the Woke Industrial Complex on social justice discourse also extends to academic and educational settings. The movement has influenced curricula, prompting discussions about the inclusion of diverse perspectives and histories in education.

The Woke Industrial Complex has had a multifaceted impact on social justice discourse. While it has brought important issues to the forefront and empowered grassroots activists, it has also sparked debates about language, tactics, and the commodification of social justice. By engaging in critical reflection and fostering open dialogue, the "wokeness" movement can continue to shape social justice discourse in ways that promote genuine transformation and progress.

## Navigating Authentic Activism

In the midst of the Woke Industrial Complex, navigating authentic activism becomes a crucial endeavor for individuals and movements committed to genuine social justice. As the landscape of advocacy becomes more complex, advocates must grapple with questions of authenticity, accountability, and meaningful impact. This section explores strategies for navigating authentic activism within the "wokeness" movement.

**Centering Marginalized Voices:** Authentic activism requires centering the voices and experiences of marginalized communities. Advocates must listen to and amplify the perspectives of those directly impacted by systemic injustice. This involves recognizing the intersectionality of different forms of oppression and ensuring that advocacy efforts are inclusive and empowering.

**Substantive Action over Performative Gestures:** Rather than engaging in empty symbolism, authentic activism emphasizes substantive action. This means advocating for systemic change and addressing root causes of oppression. Advocates must go beyond surface-level gestures and demand meaningful policies and practices that promote equity and justice.

**Transparency and Accountability:** Transparency is essential in navigating authentic activism. Advocates should be open about their goals, strategies, and the impact of their efforts. Accountability measures, such as regular evaluations and reporting, can help ensure that advocacy remains aligned with its stated values.

**Critical Reflection:** Authentic activism requires constant reflection and learning. Advocates must be open to feedback and willing to critically assess their own biases and blind spots. This continuous learning process helps to refine advocacy efforts and ensures that they remain relevant and effective.

**Building Genuine Alliances:** Collaboration and coalition-building are central to authentic activism. Building genuine alliances with other social justice movements and grassroots organizations strengthens collective impact and fosters a more inclusive and intersectional approach to advocacy.

**Prioritizing Impact Over Image:** While visibility is essential in advocacy, the focus should remain on meaningful impact rather than cultivating a certain image. Advocates must resist the allure of performative activism and prioritize creating tangible and sustainable change.

**Resisting Co-optation:** Navigating authentic activism requires vigilance against co-optation by powerful actors, including corporations and politicians. Advocates must resist being co-opted or manipulated into supporting causes that do not align with the movement's transformative goals.

**Embracing Complexity:** Social justice issues are multifaceted and complex. Authentic activism acknowledges this complexity and avoids simplistic or reductionist approaches. Advocates must be willing to engage with nuance and uncertainty, recognizing that there are no easy solutions to deeply rooted systemic problems.

Navigating authentic activism within the Woke Industrial Complex demands intentionality, humility, and a commitment to genuine social justice. By centering marginalized voices, prioritizing substantive action, and fostering genuine alliances, advocates can work towards transformative change that challenges systemic oppression. As the "wokeness" movement continues to evolve, embracing authentic activism is crucial for achieving lasting impact and meaningful progress.

The Woke Industrial Complex is a dynamic and multifaceted phenomenon that has reshaped the landscape of social justice advocacy. As the movement continues to evolve, it brings both opportunities and challenges to the pursuit of equity, justice, and systemic change. This section provides a concluding reflection on the Woke Industrial Complex and its impact on the "wokeness" movement.

The rise of the Woke Industrial Complex has undoubtedly brought critical social justice issues to the forefront of public consciousness. It has amplified the voices of marginalized communities, sparked important conversations, and empowered grassroots activism. Through social media, digital platforms, and the commercialization of "wokeness," the movement has reached new heights of visibility and engagement.

However, this increased visibility has also given rise to concerns about authenticity, co-optation, and performative activism. The commodification of social justice issues by corporations, politicians, and influencers has led to debates about the sincerity of their engagement. Moreover, the use of social justice language as a branding strategy raises questions about the impact of "wokeness" marketing on genuine transformative change.

The Woke Industrial Complex has also faced internal critiques about the potential for cancel culture, the effectiveness of language and tactics, and the need for deeper systemic change. Advocates within the "wokeness" movement are engaged in ongoing discussions about how to navigate these challenges while remaining true to the movement's transformative goals.

To ensure the authenticity and effectiveness of the "wokeness" movement, advocates must prioritize genuine action over surface-level gestures. Substantive policy changes, intersectional approaches, and building genuine alliances are essential for addressing the root causes of systemic oppression.

Furthermore, the movement must guard against co-optation and resist being co-opted for commercial or political gain. Advocates must hold powerful actors accountable for their actions and demand transparency in their commitments to social justice causes.

Navigating authentic activism within the Woke Industrial Complex requires critical reflection, humility, and a commitment to learning and growth. By centering the voices and experiences of marginalized communities and prioritizing substantive impact over image, advocates can maintain the movement's integrity and drive meaningful progress.

The Woke Industrial Complex is a double-edged sword that presents both opportunities and challenges to the "wokeness" movement. While it has brought important social justice issues to the forefront, it has also prompted debates about authenticity and performative activism. By engaging in continuous learning, building genuine alliances, and prioritizing meaningful action, the "wokeness" movement can navigate the complexities of the Woke Industrial Complex and continue its pursuit of equity and justice.

*"In the hands of the unscrupulous, 'woke' became a weapon to bludgeon reason into submission and a detonator for mass distraction."*

# CHAPTER 5
# THE WEAPONIZATION OF "WOKE"

The term "woke," once a term embraced by activists fighting for justice, has now become a contentious battleground in the cultural and political spheres. The Weaponization of "Woke" explores how this once empowering term has been appropriated, distorted, and deployed as a rhetorical weapon, often devoid of its original meaning and intention.

The term "woke" emerged from the Black community's long-standing struggle against systemic racism and injustice. It signified being awake to the pervasive discrimination faced by marginalized communities and acknowledging the need for collective action to address these issues. However, in the era of the Woke Industrial Complex, the term has been co-opted, stripped of its authentic context, and used as a tool to attack progressive causes and social justice advocates.

One of the most significant ways "woke" has been weaponized is through its adoption by conservative and right-wing groups. These groups have sought to redefine and twist the term's meaning to discredit progressive movements and portray advocates as overly politically correct or divisive. By framing "woke" as an excessive and irrational pursuit of social justice, they aim to undermine efforts to address systemic inequalities.

Furthermore, the weaponization of "woke" has become part of a broader culture war, with various media outlets, politicians, and interest groups using the term to fuel ideological divisions. In this context, the weaponization of "woke" serves as a political strategy to rally and mobilize certain voter bases, leveraging cultural anxieties around change and societal shifts.

The weaponization of "woke" has also been employed as a tactic to distract from legitimate social justice issues and avoid engaging with substantive concerns. By reducing complex and critical conversations about racism, sexism, and other forms of discrimination to a simple dismissal of "wokeness," genuine efforts towards equality and inclusion are stifled.

The redefinition and weaponization of "woke" have even led to backlash against diversity and inclusion initiatives in various spaces, including academia, corporations, and the arts. This backlash is fueled by a misrepresentation of "wokeness" as a threat to free speech or as a form of reverse discrimination, despite its original purpose of combating discrimination and inequality.

As we go further into this chapter, we will explore the various ways in which "woke" has been weaponized, the actors involved in this process, and the implications for social justice advocacy. Understanding the weaponization of "woke" is crucial to combatting its misuse and reaffirming the term's genuine pursuit of a more equitable and just society.

## "Woke" as a Pejorative

Inside cultural and political discourse, the term "woke" has increasingly been used as a pejorative to dismiss and belittle advocates for social justice and progressive causes. The transformation of "woke" from a term of empowerment to a derogatory label is emblematic of the weaponization it has undergone. This section examines the ways in which "woke" has become a pejorative and its impact on social justice advocacy.

One of the primary mechanisms through which "woke" has become a pejorative is through its association with excessive political correctness and perceived hypersensitivity. Critics of social justice movements use "woke" as a shorthand for what they consider to be an overzealous pursuit of language and behavior policing. They argue that it stifles free speech and curtails open dialogue by creating a fear of saying the "wrong" thing.

Moreover, the term has been weaponized to frame social justice advocates as self-righteous and morally superior. By labeling someone as "woke," critics imply that they are excessively virtuous and condescending, looking down upon those who do not share their views. This portrayal seeks to delegitimize the authenticity and sincerity of social justice advocacy.

The "woke" pejorative is also used to perpetuate stereotypes about progressive activists. It is often deployed to caricature advocates as naïve, unrealistic, and disconnected from the complexities of real-world challenges. This misrepresentation obscures the substantive goals of social justice movements and undermines the serious issues they seek to address.

Furthermore, the pejorative use of "woke" has become a rhetorical strategy in political debates. Critics may use it to dismiss arguments and concerns raised by progressive voices without engaging with the substantive content of their positions. By reducing complex issues to a derogatory label, they sidestep the need to address the merits of the social justice claims.

The weaponization of "woke" as a pejorative has significant implications for social justice advocacy. It can discourage individuals from publicly expressing support for progressive causes, as they may fear being labeled as "woke" and facing ridicule or backlash. It can also create a chilling effect on critical discussions about race, gender, and other forms of discrimination, hindering progress towards greater equality and inclusion.

Moreover, the "woke" pejorative can deepen ideological divisions and polarize public discourse. It fosters a hostile environment where nuanced conversations about social justice are replaced with ad hominem attacks and character assassination.

The transformation of "woke" into a pejorative reflects the weaponization of the term to undermine and discredit social justice advocacy. By framing "woke" as excessive, self-righteous, and censorious, critics aim to dismiss the legitimate concerns and goals of progressive movements. Recognizing the pejorative use of "woke" is crucial for countering its negative impact on social justice discourse and reclaiming the term's original commitment to equity, inclusivity, and justice.

## The "Woke" Backlash: A Political Tool

The term "woke" has become a potent political tool in the culture war, with conservative and right-wing groups leveraging its negative connotations to galvanize their base and undermine progressive causes. This section explores the "woke" backlash as a political strategy and its impact on social justice advocacy.

Conservative politicians and media outlets have strategically weaponized "woke" to tap into cultural anxieties and mobilize their supporters. By framing social justice advocacy as an existential threat to traditional values and norms, they have portrayed themselves as defenders of traditionalism and patriotism. This tactic aims to rally their base against perceived threats to the status quo, using "woke" as a symbol of excessive liberal activism.

The "woke" backlash has been particularly effective in shaping political discourse and mobilizing voters during election cycles. By positioning themselves as adversaries of "wokeness," conservative politicians have sought to attract voters who may feel alienated or threatened by social justice movements' demands for change.

Moreover, the "woke" backlash has intersected with broader debates about nationalism and identity politics. Critics of social justice movements have framed "wokeness" as divisive and exclusionary, accusing progressive advocates of perpetuating identity politics and sowing discord among different racial and cultural groups.

The "woke" backlash as a political tool has also manifested in the form of legislative efforts and policy proposals. Some politicians have sought to restrict diversity and inclusion training, limit discussions about systemic racism, or ban the teaching of critical race theory in schools. These actions are often justified by framing "wokeness" as a threat to national unity or as an attempt to indoctrinate children with radical ideologies.

As a political tool, the "woke" backlash has implications for social justice advocacy. It can lead to the stigmatization and suppression of progressive voices, hindering efforts to address systemic inequities and discrimination. It may also foster a climate of fear and reluctance to engage in critical conversations about race, gender, and other forms of social justice.

Furthermore, the "woke" backlash diverts attention from substantive issues and obscures the real-world challenges faced by marginalized communities. By framing social justice movements as a distraction from "real" problems, conservative actors avoid engaging with systemic issues and hinder progress towards more inclusive and equitable societies.

The "woke" backlash serves as a potent political tool in the culture war, mobilizing conservative support and undermining progressive causes. By framing "wokeness" as a threat to traditional values and national unity, conservative groups seek to galvanize their base and position themselves as defenders of the status quo. Understanding the "woke" backlash as a political strategy is essential for social justice advocates to effectively address the challenges posed by its negative impact on discourse and policy.

## Polarization and Identity Politics

The weaponization of "woke" has fueled the flames of polarization and identity politics, further dividing societies along ideological lines. This section explores how the misuse of "woke" as a pejorative and a political tool has contributed to the intensification of polarization and the rise of identity-based political movements.

The weaponization of "woke" has deepened ideological divides by framing social justice advocacy as a threat to traditional values and a radical departure from mainstream beliefs. This portrayal fosters a binary view of the world, pitting those who embrace social justice issues against those who view them as a threat to established norms. As a result, discussions about equity, inclusion, and justice become increasingly polarized, leaving little room for nuanced and productive dialogue.

Furthermore, the weaponization of "woke" has been accompanied by the rise of identity-based political movements, both on the left and the right. Critics of social justice movements often accuse them of perpetuating identity politics, while advocates argue that acknowledging and addressing identity-based oppression is essential for transformative change.

The weaponization of "woke" has also led to a backlash against intersectionality, a framework that recognizes how different forms of oppression intersect and compound. Critics of social justice movements often reject intersectionality as a divisive approach that prioritizes identity over shared values and experiences. This rejection further hinders the understanding of how multiple systems of oppression intertwine and perpetuate each other.

In addition, the weaponization of "woke" has contributed to the erasure of the experiences and struggles of marginalized communities. By framing social justice advocates as "woke" warriors detached from reality, critics undermine the validity of lived experiences and the need for addressing systemic injustices.

The polarization and identity politics intensified by the weaponization of "woke" have implications for social justice advocacy. Meaningful progress towards equity and justice requires bridging ideological divides and finding common ground on shared values. By weaponizing "woke," these divides are further entrenched, making it challenging to build broad-based alliances for transformative change.

Moreover, the weaponization of "woke" can distract from substantive issues, leading to a focus on labels and identities rather than the concrete policy changes necessary for dismantling systemic discrimination. This fixation on ideological differences can hinder collective action to address pressing social issues.

The weaponization of "woke" has contributed to the polarization and identity politics that are pervasive in contemporary societies. By framing social justice advocacy as a threat to traditional values and promoting a binary view of the world, the misuse of "woke" further divides societies along ideological lines. Recognizing the impact of the weaponization of "woke" on polarization and identity politics is crucial for fostering more constructive dialogue and effective social justice advocacy.

### Silencing Dissent and Debates

The weaponization of "woke" has had a chilling effect on dissent and critical debates, undermining the principles of free speech and open dialogue. This section examines how the misuse of "woke" as a pejorative and a political tool has led to the suppression of dissenting voices and stifled substantive discussions.

One of the consequences of the weaponization of "woke" is the creation of a hostile environment for those who express dissenting views. Individuals who question certain aspects of social justice movements or challenge prevailing narratives may fear being labeled as "anti-woke" and face public shaming or even threats to their careers and reputations.

Moreover, the misuse of "woke" as a pejorative has led to a distortion of free speech debates. Critics of social justice movements often use the term to argue that "cancel culture" and "political correctness" are undermining free expression. However, this portrayal overlooks the power dynamics at play, where marginalized voices often face severe consequences for expressing their views.

The weaponization of "woke" has also hindered substantive debates about social justice issues. By reducing complex discussions to simplistic accusations of being "woke" or "anti-woke," genuine engagement with the nuances of systemic discrimination and potential solutions is stifled.

Furthermore, the weaponization of "woke" as a political tool has led to a polarization of public discourse, where differing views on social justice are portrayed as irreconcilable and incompatible. This polarization discourages meaningful conversations and collaborative efforts to address societal challenges.

The weaponization of "woke" has also impacted academia, where the fear of being labeled "woke" or "politically correct" can discourage scholars from pursuing research on sensitive topics or from presenting findings that challenge prevailing narratives.

Additionally, the weaponization of "woke" has created a reluctance among some to engage in self-reflection and critical examination of their own beliefs and actions. Fear of being labeled as "woke" or "virtue signaling" can lead to a defensive posture, hindering personal growth and collective learning.

The weaponization of "woke" has had detrimental effects on dissent and debates, undermining the principles of free speech and open dialogue. The misuse of "woke" as a pejorative and a political tool has created a hostile environment for dissenting voices and stifled substantive discussions about social justice issues. Addressing the silencing of dissent and debates is essential for fostering a more inclusive and constructive public discourse.

## The "Wokeness" Red Herring

The weaponization of "woke" has given rise to what can be described as the "wokeness" red herring - a distraction tactic that diverts attention from substantive social justice issues by focusing on exaggerated or mischaracterized instances of "wokeness." This section explores how the "wokeness" red herring is employed as a rhetorical strategy to undermine the legitimacy of social justice movements.

Critics of social justice advocacy often cherry-pick extreme or fringe examples of "wokeness" to portray the entire movement as irrational and detached from reality. By highlighting instances of overzealous language policing or extreme demands, they create a distorted narrative that misrepresents the broader goals and concerns of social justice movements.

The "wokeness" red herring is frequently used as a way to dismiss the need for addressing systemic injustices. Critics argue that focusing on exaggerated instances of "wokeness" distracts from more pressing issues such as economic inequality or crime rates. This tactic disregards the fact that social justice movements are often simultaneously addressing multiple forms of oppression and seeking holistic societal change.

Moreover, the "wokeness" red herring is employed to delegitimize the very notion of social justice. By reducing the complex and nuanced pursuit of equity and inclusivity to a caricature of hypersensitivity, critics aim to undermine the moral foundation of social justice advocacy.

The "wokeness" red herring also obscures the genuine progress made by social justice movements in advancing civil rights and promoting diversity and inclusion. Critics often downplay or ignore the positive impacts of social justice advocacy, focusing solely on instances that can be sensationalized or misconstrued.

Additionally, the "wokeness" red herring can create a false equivalency between social justice movements and other forms of extremism.

By associating "wokeness" with radical ideologies or cult-like behavior, critics attempt to discredit the serious and well-reasoned arguments put forth by social justice advocates.

The "wokeness" red herring ultimately hampers meaningful conversations about the pressing social issues that social justice movements seek to address. Instead of engaging with the complexities of systemic discrimination and structural inequality, attention is diverted to exaggerated portrayals of "wokeness."

The "wokeness" red herring is a rhetorical strategy employed by critics of social justice movements to undermine their legitimacy and distract from substantive issues. By focusing on extreme or fringe examples of "wokeness," critics misrepresent the broader goals and concerns of social justice advocacy. Recognizing and addressing the "wokeness" red herring is crucial for fostering more constructive and informed discussions about the challenges and opportunities of creating a more just and equitable society.

## The Intersection with Free Speech

The weaponization of "woke" has ignited complex debates at the intersection of "wokeness" and free speech. As the term is increasingly used as a pejorative to silence dissent and stifle critical discussions, questions arise about how to navigate the delicate balance between safeguarding free expression and fostering inclusive and respectful discourse.

At its core, free speech is a fundamental democratic value that ensures individuals have the right to express their ideas and opinions without censorship or punishment by the government. However, the weaponization of "woke" has extended the debate beyond government restrictions, as private actors such as corporations, social media platforms, and institutions have become significant players in shaping public discourse.

Critics argue that the weaponization of "woke" is eroding free speech by creating a climate of self-censorship. Individuals may refrain from expressing their opinions or engaging in open debates due to the fear of being labeled as "anti-woke" or facing social repercussions. This chilling effect can hinder the robust exchange of ideas that is essential for a vibrant and democratic society.

On the other hand, proponents of social justice advocacy emphasize the importance of creating safe and inclusive spaces where marginalized voices can be heard without fear of harassment or harm. They argue that protecting free speech should not mean allowing hate speech or discriminatory rhetoric to go unchecked. Instead, it should involve actively countering such speech while promoting a culture of respect and empathy.

Navigating the intersection of "wokeness" and free speech also raises questions about the responsibilities of social media platforms and corporations in moderating content. Some argue that these private entities should be more transparent and consistent in their content policies to avoid inadvertently stifling free expression. Others contend that platform owners have a duty to address hate speech and misinformation to protect users from harmful content.

Furthermore, the weaponization of "woke" intersects with debates about academic freedom and intellectual diversity on college campuses. Calls for "safe spaces" and "trigger warnings" are often criticized as impinging on free speech, while advocates argue that these measures are necessary to foster an inclusive learning environment.

The weaponization of "woke" has sparked intricate discussions about the intersection of "wokeness" and free speech. Balancing the protection of free expression with the need for respectful and inclusive discourse is a challenging task in an era where private actors wield significant influence over public discussions. Navigating this intersection requires thoughtful considerations of the responsibilities of individuals, institutions, and corporations in fostering robust debates while combatting harmful speech.

## The Impact on Social Justice Movements

The weaponization of "woke" has had a profound impact on social justice movements, influencing their strategies, public perception, and internal dynamics. This section explores how the misuse of "woke" as a pejorative and a political tool has shaped the trajectory of social justice advocacy.

One significant impact of the weaponization of "woke" is the delegitimization of social justice movements in the eyes of some segments of the public. By framing advocates as "woke warriors" engaged in extreme and irrational behavior, critics undermine the credibility and seriousness of the issues being addressed.

The weaponization of "woke" has also led to a form of backlash against social justice movements, with some individuals becoming resistant to engaging with the principles of equity and inclusion. This resistance can hinder the progress of social justice initiatives and the building of coalitions necessary for meaningful change.

Moreover, the weaponization of "woke" can create divisions within social justice movements themselves. Differences of opinion about the meaning and application of "woke" principles can lead to internal conflicts, diverting energy away from collective goals.

The impact of the weaponization of "woke" on social justice movements is particularly evident in online spaces, where debates about social issues often take place. Social media platforms have become battlegrounds for these discussions, with the weaponization of "woke" exacerbating polarization and the tendency to engage in adversarial debates.

Furthermore, the weaponization of "woke" has resulted in some activists distancing themselves from the term and seeking alternative language to articulate their goals. This shift in language is an attempt to avoid the negative associations and stereotypes associated with "wokeness" and to refocus the narrative on substantive issues.

The weaponization of "woke" has also influenced how some social justice organizations approach advocacy and communication. They may strategically adjust their messaging to anticipate and counter criticisms related to "wokeness," emphasizing the pragmatic and evidence-based nature of their work.

Additionally, the weaponization of "woke" has highlighted the need for continuous self-reflection within social justice movements. Leaders and activists must critically examine their approaches and strategies to ensure they remain inclusive, open to dialogue, and focused on meaningful change.

The weaponization of "woke" has had a significant impact on social justice movements, affecting their credibility, public perception, and internal dynamics. As critics misrepresent the goals and principles of social justice advocacy, movement leaders must navigate these challenges while staying committed to their vision for a more equitable and just society. Addressing the impact of the weaponization of "woke" is essential for social justice movements to continue advancing their objectives and building a broad-based coalition for transformative change.

### The Role of Media and Information Warfare

The weaponization of "woke" has become intertwined with media and information warfare, where the dissemination and distortion of information are leveraged to advance certain narratives and political agendas. This section explores how media platforms and actors play a pivotal role in perpetuating the weaponization of "woke" and shaping public opinion.

Social media platforms have become battlegrounds for information warfare, with the weaponization of "woke" often at the center of these conflicts. Partisan actors and ideological groups use social media to amplify and propagate narratives that misrepresent social justice movements as irrational, divisive, and extremist.

In many instances, disinformation campaigns deliberately amplify extreme examples of "wokeness" to create a distorted image of social justice advocacy. These campaigns exploit confirmation bias and emotional reactions to deepen social divides and erode trust in the legitimacy of social justice movements.

Moreover, the weaponization of "woke" is often employed as a divisive tactic in broader political struggles. By framing social justice advocates as "woke warriors," critics can create a false binary where supporting social justice becomes synonymous with "cancel culture" or "virtue signaling," thus undermining the broader principles of equity and inclusion.

The rise of "echo chambers" and "filter bubbles" on social media platforms further exacerbates the weaponization of "woke." Algorithmic recommendation systems can reinforce users' exposure to like-minded perspectives, leading to a reinforcement of existing beliefs and further polarization.

Media outlets, both mainstream and partisan, also play a significant role in perpetuating the weaponization of "woke." Sensationalized headlines and clickbait articles that focus on extreme examples of "wokeness" can distort the public's understanding of social justice movements.

Additionally, the weaponization of "woke" can become a topic of discussion in mainstream news outlets, where pundits and commentators contribute to the polarization by framing debates about social justice as "culture wars."

The use of "wokeness" as a political wedge issue is evident in political campaigns and elections. Candidates and political organizations may strategically employ the term to appeal to specific voter bases or to discredit opponents.

To address the role of media and information warfare in the weaponization of "woke," it is essential to prioritize media literacy and critical thinking. Individuals must be equipped to recognize disinformation and be mindful of the ways in which media narratives can shape public perception.

The weaponization of "woke" is deeply intertwined with media and information warfare, where narratives are exploited and distorted to serve particular agendas. Social media platforms, mainstream media, and political actors all play pivotal roles in perpetuating the weaponization of "woke" and shaping public opinion. Recognizing and confronting the impact of media and information warfare is crucial for fostering a more informed and constructive public discourse about social justice issues.

## Navigating a Constructive Discourse

Amid the weaponization of "woke," navigating a constructive discourse becomes essential for promoting understanding, empathy, and meaningful dialogue about social justice issues. This section explores strategies to address the challenges posed by the misuse of "woke" and foster productive conversations.

**Promoting Media Literacy:** Media literacy education is crucial for empowering individuals to discern reliable information from disinformation and propaganda. Teaching critical thinking skills and encouraging fact-checking can help individuals become more discerning consumers of information.

**Encouraging Civil Discourse:** Fostering an environment of civil discourse is paramount to facilitating open and respectful discussions. Emphasizing active listening, empathy, and respect for differing viewpoints can help reduce polarization and encourage constructive engagement.

**Centering Intersectionality:** Recognizing the interconnectedness of various forms of oppression and privilege is vital for effective social justice advocacy. An intersectional approach acknowledges that individuals experience multiple dimensions of identity and marginalization.

**Amplifying Marginalized Voices:** Elevating the voices of marginalized communities is crucial to ensure their perspectives are heard and understood. Centering their experiences in discussions about social justice helps counter the mischaracterizations perpetuated by the weaponization of "woke."

**Engaging in Dialogue, Not Monologue:** Moving away from monologue-style communication and embracing genuine dialogue can lead to more productive conversations. Emphasizing collaboration and shared learning can foster connections and promote understanding.

**Addressing Legitimate Concerns:** Acknowledging and addressing legitimate concerns about social justice movements can build bridges with skeptics. Demonstrating a willingness to engage in constructive self-critique and growth enhances the credibility of social justice advocacy.

**Seeking Common Ground:** Identifying shared goals and values can create opportunities for cooperation and collaboration. Finding common ground on issues such as economic inequality or access to education can serve as a starting point for constructive dialogue.

**Challenging False Narratives:** Confronting and challenging false narratives about "wokeness" is essential for countering the weaponization of the term. Promoting accurate and nuanced information about social justice movements can help dispel stereotypes and misrepresentations.

**Promoting Restorative Justice:** Emphasizing the principles of restorative justice over punitive measures can create spaces for healing and reconciliation. Focusing on dialogue and understanding can lead to transformative change instead of perpetuating divisions.

**Building Coalitions:** Creating broad-based coalitions that encompass diverse perspectives can strengthen social justice movements. Engaging with individuals who may not fully embrace "wokeness" but share common goals can lead to more inclusive and effective advocacy.

Navigating a constructive discourse in the face of the weaponization of "woke" is crucial for promoting understanding, empathy, and transformative change. Emphasizing media literacy, civil discourse, intersectionality, and amplifying marginalized voices can counter the harmful effects of misrepresentations and promote more informed discussions about social justice issues. By engaging in genuine dialogue, addressing concerns, and seeking common ground, we can build bridges and work towards a more just and equitable society. In the subsequent sections, we will delve further into the multifaceted implications of the weaponization of "woke" for social justice advocacy.

The weaponization of "woke" represents a complex and multifaceted phenomenon that has significant implications for social justice advocacy and public discourse. In this chapter, we have explored the various ways in which "wokeness" has been misappropriated and manipulated as a pejorative term to undermine social justice movements and stifle progressive change. We have examined how the misuse of "woke" has permeated media and information warfare, fueled polarization, and impacted the pursuit of authentic activism.

The weaponization of "woke" is not just a linguistic battle; it reflects deeper societal tensions surrounding identity, power, and systemic inequalities. The co-optation of "wokeness" by corporations, political actors, and media outlets has created an environment where the pursuit of social justice is often reduced to performative gestures, tokenism, and divisive tactics.

As we navigate the challenges posed by the weaponization of "woke," it is crucial to maintain a focus on the core principles of social justice advocacy: equity, inclusion, and empathy. Elevating marginalized voices, practicing active listening, and engaging in respectful dialogue can help foster understanding and build bridges across ideological divides.

Moreover, it is essential to recognize that the weaponization of "woke" is just one facet of a broader struggle for social change. True progress requires a comprehensive understanding of the intersections between various forms of oppression and privilege. An inclusive and intersectional approach to activism can lead to more meaningful and sustainable change.

Within this climate of weaponization, it becomes imperative to refrain from succumbing to the allure of engaging in adversarial debates. Instead, we must seek common ground and work towards finding shared solutions to the pressing social issues we face.

To counter the harmful effects of the weaponization of "woke," media literacy education and critical thinking are essential. Empowering individuals to navigate the complex landscape of information and disinformation can help build a more informed and discerning public.

Addressing the weaponization of "woke" requires a collective effort from activists, media professionals, educators, and policymakers. By centering authentic advocacy, promoting constructive discourse, and challenging false narratives, we can reclaim the narrative surrounding "wokeness" and refocus on the urgent work of creating a more just and equitable society for all.

*"Being 'woke' means not only seeing the cracks in the facade of equality
but also dismantling the very structures that uphold them."*

# CHAPTER 6
# UNPACKING STRUCTURAL RACISM

The unpacking of structural racism is a critical endeavor in understanding the deep-rooted and systemic inequalities that persist in contemporary societies. Structural racism refers to the ways in which societal institutions, policies, and practices perpetuate racial disparities, often resulting in marginalized communities facing greater barriers to opportunities and resources.

While overt expressions of racism have been challenged over time, structural racism remains insidious, operating beneath the surface of daily life and perpetuating disparities across multiple domains, including education, housing, healthcare, and the criminal justice system.

In this chapter, we scrutinize the multifaceted nature of structural racism, examining its historical roots, manifestations, and consequences. We will explore the ways in which systems and institutions have been shaped by historical discrimination and how these legacies continue to shape present-day disparities.

Understanding structural racism requires grappling with complex and interconnected factors. Historical practices such as slavery, colonialism, and segregation have left lasting imprints on societal structures, and these legacies continue to influence outcomes for marginalized communities today.

We will also explore the ways in which policies and practices, often framed as neutral or colorblind, can perpetuate racial disparities. Colorblind approaches fail to address the unique challenges faced by marginalized communities, leading to unequal outcomes and opportunities.

Moreover, we will examine how implicit biases and stereotypes can shape decision-making within institutions, perpetuating unequal treatment and reinforcing systemic inequities.

Unpacking structural racism is not solely an intellectual exercise; it is a necessary step towards dismantling systems of oppression and working towards a more just and equitable society. By critically examining the ways in which racism operates at the structural level, we can begin to develop solutions that address root causes and challenge the status quo.

In this chapter, we will also highlight the importance of intersectionality in understanding structural racism. Intersectionality recognizes that individuals can experience multiple forms of oppression based on their intersecting identities, such as race, gender, class, and sexuality. Understanding how these intersecting identities shape experiences of racism is crucial for developing comprehensive and effective strategies for change.

As we embark on this exploration of structural racism, we must approach the topic with humility and a commitment to learning from the experiences of those who have been most impacted. By centering the voices and perspectives of marginalized communities, we can gain a deeper understanding of the lived realities of structural racism and work towards dismantling these entrenched systems of inequity.

## Understanding Systemic Inequities

Systemic inequities lie at the heart of structural racism, perpetuating disparities and barriers that hinder the full participation and advancement of marginalized communities. This section delves into the mechanisms through which systemic inequities operate, shaping various aspects of life and reinforcing racial disparities.

**Historical Foundations:** Systemic inequities have deep historical roots, originating from centuries of slavery, colonialism, and racial segregation. These historical practices have had enduring effects, creating a foundation upon which contemporary structures of inequality are built.

**Education Disparities:** Systemic inequities are evident in educational systems, where marginalized communities often face underfunded schools, fewer opportunities for advanced coursework, and discriminatory disciplinary practices. These disparities perpetuate cycles of intergenerational poverty and limit access to higher education and better economic prospects.

**Housing Segregation:** The legacy of discriminatory housing policies, such as redlining and racially restrictive covenants, continues to impact residential segregation. Marginalized communities are disproportionately affected, facing limited access to safe and affordable housing and living in areas with inadequate resources and services.

**Healthcare Disparities:** Systemic inequities manifest in healthcare, where marginalized communities experience lower quality care, reduced access to healthcare facilities, and higher rates of chronic illnesses. These disparities have been amplified during public health crises, as seen in the disproportionate impact of COVID-19 on communities of color.

**Criminal Justice System:** The criminal justice system reflects systemic inequities through racially biased policing, harsher sentencing for people of color, and the overrepresentation of Black and Brown individuals in prisons. These inequities perpetuate a cycle of mass incarceration and hinder efforts at rehabilitation and reintegration.

**Employment and Economic Disparities:** Marginalized communities often face barriers in accessing quality job opportunities, fair wages, and career advancement. Discrimination in hiring practices and workplace policies further exacerbate economic disparities.

**Environmental Justice:** Systemic inequities are evident in environmental policies that disproportionately burden communities of color with pollution and environmental hazards. The lack of access to green spaces and clean environments can negatively impact health outcomes.

**Political Representation:** Marginalized communities often face barriers in political participation and representation, leading to limited influence in decision-making processes and policies that affect them.

Understanding systemic inequities is essential for dismantling structural racism. It requires acknowledging that racial disparities are not the result of individual shortcomings but rather the outcome of deeply entrenched systems and policies. Solutions to address systemic inequities must be comprehensive, tackling root causes and dismantling barriers that hinder progress and perpetuate disparities. An intersectional approach that recognizes the interconnectedness of various forms of oppression is crucial for developing effective strategies that foster a more equitable and just society.

## The Role of Historical Context

To comprehend the intricacies of structural racism, it is imperative to recognize the profound impact of historical context on shaping contemporary inequities. Historical events and policies have left indelible imprints on societal structures, perpetuating racial disparities and systemic racism in the present day.

**Legacy of Slavery:** The transatlantic slave trade and centuries of enslavement of Black people laid the foundation for structural racism in the United States and other parts of the world. The enduring effects of slavery can be seen in the wealth gap, educational disparities, and the overrepresentation of Black individuals in the criminal justice system.

**Colonialism and Its Aftermath:** Colonialism subjected indigenous populations and people of color to exploitation, dispossession of land, and cultural erasure. The consequences of colonial policies continue to shape present-day inequalities, particularly in areas with large indigenous and Black populations.

**Jim Crow Laws and Segregation:** The era of Jim Crow laws enforced racial segregation and disenfranchisement of Black Americans. While these laws have been officially dismantled, their repercussions continue to be felt in housing, education, and voting rights.

**Redlining and Housing Discrimination:** In the mid-20th century, redlining and racially restrictive covenants systematically denied Black individuals access to homeownership and relegated them to segregated neighborhoods. The lasting impact of these discriminatory practices can still be observed in today's housing disparities.

**Civil Rights Movement:** The Civil Rights Movement of the 1950s and 1960s challenged legal segregation and institutional racism, leading to significant advancements in civil rights legislation. However, the struggle for racial equality continues as systemic racism persists in various forms.

**Mass Incarceration:** The "War on Drugs" and tough-on-crime policies of the late 20th century disproportionately targeted communities of color, resulting in the mass incarceration of Black and Brown individuals. This has led to a broken criminal justice system, perpetuating cycles of poverty and disenfranchisement.

**Immigration Policies:** Discriminatory immigration policies and xenophobia have disproportionately impacted immigrant communities of color, contributing to their marginalization and limited access to resources.

Understanding the historical context of structural racism is crucial because it helps us recognize that present-day disparities do not emerge in a vacuum. They are deeply rooted in historical injustices and systemic discrimination that have endured across generations. Addressing structural racism requires acknowledging historical legacies and their role in shaping contemporary inequities.

Moreover, historical context reminds us that the fight against racism is an ongoing struggle that demands sustained efforts to dismantle entrenched systems of inequality. Recognizing the historical roots of structural racism empowers us to challenge the status quo, advocating for transformative policies and initiatives that address root causes rather than just symptoms.

### Implicit Bias and Discrimination

Implicit bias plays a significant role in perpetuating structural racism, influencing decision-making processes within institutions and perpetuating discriminatory practices. These biases, often unconscious, are shaped by societal stereotypes and prejudices, leading to unequal treatment and outcomes for marginalized communities.

**Understanding Implicit Bias:** Implicit biases are attitudes and beliefs that individuals hold unconsciously, often outside of their awareness. These biases can be shaped by societal messages, media portrayals, and cultural narratives. They may influence how individuals perceive and interact with others, leading to unintentional discrimination.

**Impact on Decision-Making:** Implicit biases can affect decision-making in various domains, including hiring practices, education, law enforcement, and healthcare. For example, studies have shown that job applicants with names perceived as "Black-sounding" are less likely to be called for interviews, even when their qualifications are identical to those with "White-sounding" names.

**Educational Settings:** Implicit biases can manifest in educational settings, where students of color may face lower expectations from educators, leading to reduced academic opportunities and outcomes. Biased disciplinary practices can also contribute to the school-to-prison pipeline for students of color.

**Policing and Criminal Justice:** Implicit biases can influence law enforcement interactions, leading to racial profiling and biased policing practices. This contributes to the disproportionate targeting and incarceration of Black and Brown individuals.

**Healthcare Disparities:** Implicit biases in healthcare settings can result in differential treatment, misdiagnoses, and inadequate care for patients of color. This can lead to poorer health outcomes and exacerbate existing healthcare disparities.

**Legal System:** Implicit biases can impact legal decisions, from jury selection to sentencing, leading to unequal treatment and perpetuating systemic racism within the justice system.

**Intersectionality:** The impacts of implicit bias can be compounded for individuals who belong to multiple marginalized groups. Intersectionality, which recognizes the interconnectedness of various forms of oppression, highlights the complex ways in which individuals experience discrimination based on their intersecting identities.

Recognizing and addressing implicit biases is critical for dismantling structural racism. Institutions must implement policies and training programs to raise awareness of implicit bias and mitigate its impact on decision-making. Additionally, promoting diversity and representation within institutions can help challenge biases and foster more inclusive environments.

Furthermore, fostering dialogue and empathy among individuals from diverse backgrounds can help bridge divides and promote understanding. By actively challenging stereotypes and engaging in self-reflection, individuals can work to counteract the effects of implicit bias.

One must embrace the imperative of confronting implicit bias while simultaneously engaging in broader endeavors to combat systemic racism. As we continue to unpack structural racism, we must recognize the role that implicit bias plays in perpetuating discrimination and inequality, striving towards a more equitable society for all.

## Criminal Justice and Mass Incarceration

The criminal justice system in many countries, including the United States, has become a powerful driver of structural racism, perpetuating racial disparities and contributing to mass incarceration. This section examines the ways in which the criminal justice system intersects with structural racism and how it has resulted in a disproportionately high number of people of color being incarcerated.

**Racial Profiling:** Racial profiling, a form of discriminatory law enforcement, targets individuals based on their race, ethnicity, or perceived background. This practice leads to the over-policing of Black and Brown communities, resulting in higher rates of arrests and criminal charges.

**War on Drugs:** The "War on Drugs" policies, initiated in the 1970s, disproportionately targeted communities of color, particularly Black individuals. The criminalization of drug offenses, coupled with harsh sentencing laws, contributed to the exponential growth of the prison population and exacerbated racial disparities in incarceration rates.

**Bail and Pretrial Detention:** Structural racism is evident in the pretrial stage of the criminal justice system, where individuals from marginalized communities are more likely to be held in pretrial detention due to unaffordable bail conditions. This practice further perpetuates a cycle of poverty and disadvantage.

**Sentencing Disparities:** Racial disparities are evident in sentencing practices, with people of color receiving harsher sentences for similar offenses compared to their White counterparts. Mandatory minimums and three-strikes laws have contributed to the over-representation of Black and Brown individuals in the prison system.

**School-to-Prison Pipeline:** Structural racism manifests in the school-to-prison pipeline, where punitive disciplinary practices disproportionately target students of color, leading to increased involvement with the criminal justice system.

**Parole and Reentry:** Individuals with criminal records face significant barriers to reintegration into society, such as limited job opportunities and restricted access to housing. These challenges disproportionately impact people of color, hindering their ability to rebuild their lives after incarceration.

**Prison Labor Exploitation:** Mass incarceration has led to the exploitation of prison labor, where incarcerated individuals, often from marginalized communities, are paid meager wages for their work, perpetuating a modern form of slavery.

Addressing the intersection of structural racism with the criminal justice system requires comprehensive reforms. These reforms should include revisiting sentencing laws, promoting alternatives to incarceration, investing in diversion and rehabilitation programs, and addressing the root causes of crime.

Moreover, transformative justice approaches that focus on healing and community restoration rather than punishment can be more effective in addressing the harm caused by crime and reducing recidivism rates.

In order to achieve true justice and dismantle structural racism, it is essential to confront the deeply rooted issues within the criminal justice system and work towards creating a more equitable and just society for all individuals, regardless of their race or background.

## Education Disparities

Education is often regarded as the great equalizer, providing opportunities for upward mobility and personal growth. However, structural racism profoundly impacts the education system, perpetuating disparities and hindering educational attainment for marginalized communities.

**Funding Inequities:** Funding for public schools is largely determined by local property taxes, leading to significant disparities in funding between schools in affluent neighborhoods and those in low-income communities. As a result, schools in predominantly Black and Brown neighborhoods often lack resources and struggle to provide quality education.

**School Segregation:** Despite efforts to desegregate schools, many educational institutions remain racially segregated. The persistence of de facto segregation contributes to unequal access to educational opportunities and resources.

**Disciplinary Disparities:** Black and Brown students are disproportionately subjected to harsh disciplinary practices, such as suspensions and expulsions, compared to their White peers. This contributes to the school-to-prison pipeline and hinders academic success.

**Access to Advanced Placement and Gifted Programs:** Black and Hispanic students are underrepresented in advanced placement (AP) and gifted programs, limiting their access to challenging coursework and academic opportunities.

**Culturally Relevant Education:** The curriculum in many schools often lacks representation and inclusivity, neglecting the histories and contributions of marginalized communities. Culturally relevant education is essential to validate students' identities and foster a sense of belonging.

**Access to Technology:** The digital divide exacerbates education disparities, with students in low-income communities having limited access to technology and reliable internet connections, hindering their ability to fully participate in remote learning.

**Teacher Diversity:** The teaching workforce remains predominantly White, while the student population becomes increasingly diverse. A lack of teacher diversity can hinder students' ability to connect with educators who understand their experiences and cultural backgrounds.

Addressing education disparities requires a multifaceted approach that includes equitable funding models, efforts to desegregate schools, and the implementation of culturally relevant and inclusive curricula. Moreover, providing training to educators on anti-bias and culturally responsive teaching practices is crucial to creating more inclusive learning environments.

Investing in early childhood education and providing comprehensive support services, such as mental health resources and nutrition programs, can help mitigate the effects of systemic racism on educational outcomes.

Additionally, bridging the digital divide and ensuring equitable access to technology is essential for promoting equitable learning opportunities, especially in the context of increasing reliance on digital learning platforms.

By confronting education disparities and dismantling the structures that perpetuate them, we can move closer to achieving an education system that nurtures the potential of all students, regardless of their race or socioeconomic background. Empowering students with quality education is not only an act of justice but also an investment in a more inclusive and prosperous society.

## Housing Segregation and Redlining

Housing segregation and redlining are powerful manifestations of structural racism that have profoundly shaped residential patterns and access to homeownership for marginalized communities, particularly Black Americans. These practices have had far-reaching consequences on wealth accumulation, education, and overall well-being.

**Historical Context:** Housing segregation and redlining have deep historical roots. In the early 20th century, the federal government actively promoted racial segregation through policies such as redlining, which systematically denied mortgage loans and investment to Black neighborhoods.

**Redlining and Housing Discrimination:** Redlining maps were used by banks and lending institutions to identify neighborhoods with large Black populations and then deny loans and financial services to residents in those areas. This discriminatory practice limited homeownership opportunities for Black families and perpetuated segregated communities.

**Wealth Inequity:** The denial of access to housing and homeownership resulted in a significant wealth gap between White and Black households. Homeownership is one of the most significant avenues for building intergenerational wealth, and the exclusion of Black families from this opportunity has had enduring consequences on economic mobility.

**Education and Segregation:** Housing segregation is closely linked to school segregation, as residential patterns determine school districts. Unequal funding and resources in racially segregated school districts perpetuate educational disparities for students of color.

**Health Disparities:** Housing segregation is associated with health disparities due to the concentration of pollutants and inadequate access to healthcare in marginalized communities. The stress of living in disadvantaged neighborhoods also takes a toll on physical and mental health.

**Housing Affordability:** Housing discrimination and segregation have resulted in limited affordable housing options for communities of color, leading to housing instability and homelessness.

**Current Implications:** Although redlining was officially banned in 1968, its legacy persists in the form of discriminatory lending practices and the perpetuation of racially segregated neighborhoods.

To address housing segregation and redlining, policymakers must focus on dismantling systemic barriers and promoting fair housing practices. Implementing policies that expand access to affordable housing and homeownership for marginalized communities is essential for fostering economic and social equity.

Additionally, targeted investments in historically disadvantaged neighborhoods can help revitalize communities and create more opportunities for upward mobility. Increased efforts to combat housing discrimination and increase housing affordability are crucial steps towards building more inclusive and equitable cities and towns.

Education and awareness about the history and consequences of housing segregation are also essential in fostering understanding and support for policy changes aimed at addressing this critical aspect of structural racism. By confronting the legacy of housing segregation and redlining, we can move towards building more just and equitable communities for everyone.

### Health Disparities

Structural racism profoundly impacts the health and well-being of marginalized communities, leading to significant health disparities. These disparities arise from the unequal distribution of resources, opportunities, and social determinants of health, which result in poorer health outcomes for people of color.

**Access to Healthcare:** Structural barriers, such as limited access to affordable and quality healthcare, disproportionately affect communities of color. Lack of health insurance, healthcare facilities in underserved neighborhoods, and language barriers hinder access to essential medical services.

**Social Determinants of Health:** Structural racism influences social determinants of health, including access to education, employment, housing, and nutrition. Disparities in these areas contribute to higher rates of chronic diseases, such as diabetes, heart disease, and obesity, within marginalized communities.

**Maternal and Infant Mortality:** Black women experience significantly higher rates of maternal mortality compared to White women. Structural racism contributes to inadequate prenatal care, higher rates of pregnancy-related complications, and limited access to necessary medical interventions.

**Mental Health Disparities:** The impact of structural racism on mental health is significant. Experiences of discrimination and microaggressions can lead to chronic stress and trauma, contributing to higher rates of mental health disorders among people of color.

**Environmental Racism:** Marginalized communities often face disproportionate exposure to environmental hazards, such as air pollution and toxic waste sites, due to the placement of industrial facilities and hazardous waste in their neighborhoods.

**COVID-19 Disparities:** The COVID-19 pandemic highlighted existing health disparities, as communities of color experienced higher infection rates, hospitalization rates, and death rates compared to White communities. This was exacerbated by limited access to testing, healthcare, and information.

**Implicit Bias in Healthcare:** Structural racism can also manifest in the form of implicit bias among healthcare providers, leading to differential treatment and misdiagnosis based on race.

Addressing health disparities requires a comprehensive approach that recognizes the intersectionality of social determinants of health and systemic racism. Policymakers must invest in healthcare infrastructure in underserved areas, promote diversity in the healthcare workforce, and increase cultural competency training for healthcare providers.

Moreover, policies aimed at reducing poverty, improving access to education, and providing affordable housing can have a positive impact on overall health outcomes.

Community-based interventions that address the social determinants of health and foster collaboration between healthcare providers and community organizations are also essential in narrowing health disparities.

By confronting structural racism and its impact on health, we can work towards achieving health equity and ensuring that all individuals have access to the resources and opportunities necessary to lead healthy and fulfilling lives.

## Economic Inequities

Structural racism is deeply intertwined with economic inequities, perpetuating disparities in wealth, income, and economic opportunities for communities of color. These inequities have historical roots and continue to shape economic outcomes for marginalized groups in the present day.

**Wealth Gap:** The racial wealth gap is one of the starkest manifestations of economic inequities. Historical injustices, such as slavery, redlining, and discriminatory lending practices, have hindered wealth accumulation for Black and Brown communities, leading to a significant disparity in net worth compared to White households.

**Employment Discrimination:** Marginalized communities face higher rates of employment discrimination, limiting their access to quality jobs and career advancement opportunities. Discriminatory hiring practices and wage disparities perpetuate economic inequalities.

**Occupational Segregation:** Structural racism contributes to occupational segregation, with people of color often concentrated in low-wage and precarious jobs with limited opportunities for career growth and financial stability.

**Access to Capital:** Black and Brown entrepreneurs often face challenges in accessing capital and financing for business ventures, limiting their ability to build and sustain successful businesses.

**Education and Economic Mobility:** Disparities in access to quality education hinder economic mobility for marginalized communities. Unequal funding and resources in schools perpetuate cycles of poverty and limited economic opportunities for future generations.

**Housing and Economic Opportunities:** Housing segregation and limited access to affordable housing hinder economic mobility and limit opportunities for upward social and economic mobility.

**Criminal Justice System:** Mass incarceration and over-policing in communities of color lead to long-term economic consequences, including reduced earning potential and limited employment opportunities for formerly incarcerated individuals.

**Financial Services Discrimination:** Discriminatory lending practices, such as predatory lending and redlining, have hindered access to credit and homeownership for marginalized communities.

Addressing economic inequities requires comprehensive policy solutions that address the root causes of structural racism. This includes investing in education, affordable housing, and community development programs to uplift marginalized communities and provide opportunities for economic advancement.

Furthermore, implementing fair employment practices and policies that promote diversity and inclusion in the workplace can help break down barriers to career advancement for people of color.

Policies that address the racial wealth gap, such as wealth transfer programs and reparations, are essential in rectifying historical injustices and promoting economic equity.

Economic empowerment programs that provide access to capital and technical support for minority-owned businesses can also foster entrepreneurship and economic self-sufficiency.

By dismantling the systemic barriers that perpetuate economic inequities, we can build a more just and equitable society where every individual has an opportunity to thrive and prosper, regardless of their race or background.

## Environmental Racism

Environmental racism is a form of systemic injustice where marginalized communities, particularly communities of color, bear a disproportionate burden of environmental hazards and pollution. This environmental injustice is a result of historical and ongoing policies that place hazardous facilities and toxic waste sites in or near these communities, leading to detrimental health and environmental impacts.

**Historical Roots:** Environmental racism has its roots in the historical segregation and discriminatory practices that shaped urban planning and zoning decisions. Communities of color were often forced into areas with higher pollution levels and fewer green spaces.

**Toxic Waste Sites and Industrial Facilities:** Environmental racism is evident in the placement of toxic waste sites, industrial facilities, and polluting industries in close proximity to marginalized communities. This results in increased exposure to harmful pollutants and hazardous substances, leading to health issues such as respiratory problems, cancer, and other chronic diseases.

**Air and Water Quality:** Marginalized communities often experience poorer air and water quality due to their proximity to industrial emissions and contamination. This contributes to higher rates of asthma and other respiratory illnesses in these communities.

**Climate Change Vulnerability:** Climate change exacerbates existing inequalities, with marginalized communities being more vulnerable to its impacts. They often lack resources and infrastructure to adapt to extreme weather events and rising sea levels.

**Disaster Preparedness and Recovery:** Environmental racism is evident in the lack of resources and support provided to marginalized communities during and after natural disasters. These communities often face greater challenges in disaster preparedness, response, and recovery.

**Lack of Green Spaces:** Marginalized communities often have limited access to green spaces and recreational areas, which are essential for physical and mental well-being.

**Environmental Justice Movements:** Environmental justice movements seek to address these disparities and advocate for equitable environmental policies and practices that prioritize the needs and concerns of affected communities.

To combat environmental racism, policymakers must prioritize environmental justice in decision-making processes. This includes conducting thorough environmental impact assessments and actively involving affected communities in planning and policy discussions.

Investments in sustainable and clean energy alternatives can reduce pollution and promote cleaner environments in vulnerable neighborhoods. Additionally, ensuring affordable and accessible public transportation can help mitigate environmental impacts in marginalized communities.

Furthermore, empowering communities through education and grassroots organizing can strengthen their capacity to advocate for their rights and hold polluters and policymakers accountable.

By addressing environmental racism, we can create a more sustainable and just society, where all communities have the right to live in a healthy and safe environment, regardless of their race or socioeconomic status.

## Intersectionality and Allyship

Intersectionality is a critical framework for understanding the complex and interconnected nature of various forms of oppression, including racism, sexism, homophobia, and ableism. It emphasizes that individuals can experience multiple systems of discrimination simultaneously, and their experiences are shaped by the intersections of their identities.

**Intersecting Oppressions:** Intersectionality recognizes that racism does not operate in isolation but intersects with other forms of oppression. For example, Black women may experience racism differently from Black men or White women due to the compounding effects of gender and race.

**Recognizing Privilege:** The concept of allyship is integral to addressing structural racism. White individuals, particularly those who identify as allies, must recognize and acknowledge their privilege in a racially unequal society. Allyship involves actively supporting and advocating for marginalized communities and taking responsibility for dismantling oppressive systems.

**Listening and Learning:** Allyship begins with listening and learning from the experiences and perspectives of marginalized individuals and communities. It is essential to engage in self-education about racism and its impact to better understand the structural inequalities faced by marginalized groups.

**Amplifying Marginalized Voices:** Allies can use their privilege and platforms to amplify the voices and stories of marginalized communities, providing a space for these voices to be heard and validated.

**Challenging Racism:** Allies have a responsibility to challenge racism in their personal and professional spheres. This may involve calling out racist behaviors and microaggressions, advocating for anti-racist policies, and actively working to dismantle racist systems.

**Building Solidarity:** Recognizing the interconnectedness of various forms of oppression, allies can build solidarity with other social justice movements, working collectively towards a more just and equitable society.

**Centering Marginalized Perspectives:** Intersectional allyship involves centering the experiences and perspectives of marginalized individuals and resisting the urge to dominate or co-opt movements for personal gain.

**Recognizing Mistakes and Accountability:** Allies must be willing to acknowledge and learn from their mistakes. It is essential to listen to feedback from marginalized communities and hold themselves accountable for their actions.

Intersectionality and allyship are powerful tools for dismantling structural racism. By acknowledging the complexities of oppression and recognizing the role of privilege, individuals can work together to create a society that values and celebrates the diversity of its members.

Moreover, the success of social justice movements depends on building inclusive coalitions and fostering allyship that extends beyond performative gestures. A true commitment to intersectionality and allyship requires ongoing learning, reflection, and active engagement with marginalized communities in the fight for racial justice.

Unpacking structural racism is a challenging but essential task for building a more just and equitable society. This chapter delved into the various facets of structural racism, from its historical roots to its contemporary manifestations in different areas of life. Understanding these complexities is crucial for developing effective strategies to dismantle oppressive systems and promote racial equity.

By recognizing the pervasive nature of structural racism, we acknowledge that it extends far beyond individual prejudices and biases. It is embedded in institutions, policies, and practices that have historically advantaged certain racial groups while systematically disadvantaging others.

The intersectional analysis provided insights into the interconnectedness of various forms of oppression and how they compound to create unique challenges for individuals with multiple marginalized identities. Recognizing this intersectionality is essential for creating inclusive and effective solutions to combat structural racism.

Moreover, this chapter explored the role of allyship and the importance of recognizing privilege in the fight against racism. True allyship goes beyond mere words and requires genuine action and solidarity with marginalized communities.

To address structural racism effectively, it is essential to center the experiences and voices of those most affected by it. Marginalized communities have long been at the forefront of social justice movements, advocating for change and demanding justice. Their leadership and expertise are invaluable in guiding efforts to dismantle oppressive systems.

Furthermore, this chapter highlighted the need for comprehensive policy changes that address the root causes of structural racism. From criminal justice reform to educational equity to environmental justice, systemic changes are necessary to create a more equitable society.

The fight against structural racism requires collective efforts from individuals, communities, organizations, and policymakers. It is a continuous journey that demands ongoing education, self-reflection, and a commitment to challenging oppressive systems at all levels.

By working together and holding ourselves and others accountable, we can begin to build a society that values the dignity and worth of every individual, regardless of their race or background. Unpacking structural racism is not an easy task, but it is a necessary one for achieving true racial justice and equality. Let us move forward with determination, compassion, and a vision of a more equitable and inclusive future for all.

*"It is a dagger plunged into the heart of authentic awareness."*

# CHAPTER 7
# THE QUEST FOR AUTHENTICITY

The quest for authenticity takes center stage in the pursuit of social justice and cultural transformation. As the "woke" movement continues to evolve, many individuals and communities seek to reclaim their identities, histories, and cultural expressions. This chapter investigates the multifaceted concept of authenticity and its significance in shaping social justice movements.

Authenticity encompasses a sense of genuineness, truthfulness, and alignment with one's values and beliefs. In the context of social justice, it involves embracing one's identity and experiences while challenging oppressive systems that attempt to erase or marginalize them.

One essential aspect of the quest for authenticity is the need to reclaim narratives that have been distorted or silenced by dominant powers. Marginalized communities, particularly communities of color, have often been portrayed through stereotypes and misrepresentations perpetuated by media and mainstream culture. By centering their own stories and histories, these communities reclaim agency over their identities and challenge the dominant narratives that have perpetuated racism and discrimination.

For many communities, embracing their cultural heritage is an act of resistance against cultural erasure. Colonialism and imperialism have attempted to suppress indigenous knowledge, traditions, and languages. By revitalizing and celebrating their cultural heritage, communities reclaim their authenticity and assert their right to exist on their own terms.

While authenticity is a powerful force for change, it can also be co-opted and commodified. Performative authenticity refers to instances where individuals or organizations adopt the appearance of authenticity without genuine commitment to social justice causes. This form of superficial engagement risks diluting the transformative potential of authenticity and perpetuating the very systems of oppression it aims to challenge.

Authentic allyship and solidarity require more than performative gestures or virtue signaling. Authenticity in allyship involves a genuine commitment to challenging one's privilege, actively listening to marginalized voices, and taking meaningful actions to support social justice causes.

Cultural exchange and appreciation can be enriching experiences when conducted with respect and understanding. However, it is essential to navigate the fine line between appreciation and cultural appropriation. The quest for authenticity demands sensitivity to the power dynamics at play and the potential harm caused by appropriating elements of another culture without proper acknowledgment and understanding.

Recognizing intersectionality, the interconnected nature of various forms of oppression, is crucial in the quest for authenticity. Embracing an intersectional approach means understanding that identities are multifaceted and experiences are shaped by the intersections of race, gender, class, sexuality, and more. This holistic understanding allows for more inclusive and nuanced approaches to social justice advocacy.

The quest for authenticity is not a one-size-fits-all endeavor but a complex and dynamic process that requires ongoing introspection and engagement. Embracing authenticity in social justice movements empowers individuals and communities to challenge oppressive systems, embrace their diverse identities, and build more inclusive and equitable societies.

## The Authenticity Paradox

As the pursuit of authenticity gains momentum within social justice movements, it faces a challenging paradox. On one hand, authenticity is a powerful force for positive change, empowering individuals and communities to reclaim their identities and challenge oppressive systems. On the other hand, the quest for authenticity can become a burden, demanding marginalized groups to conform to narrow and essentialist notions of their culture or experiences.

One of the key challenges in the authenticity paradox is the struggle against stereotypes. Marginalized communities have often been subjected to harmful stereotypes that reduce their identities to simplistic caricatures. In the quest for authenticity, there is a risk of essentializing these identities, reinforcing the very stereotypes that social justice movements aim to dismantle.

The pressure to embody an "authentic" identity can be overwhelming for individuals within marginalized communities. They may find themselves navigating the expectations of both their own community and the dominant society. The need to conform to a specific narrative of authenticity can stifle individuality and limit the diversity of experiences within a community.

The concept of authenticity can also be weaponized as a tool of gatekeeping within social justice spaces. Some individuals or groups may use authenticity as a means to determine who belongs to a community or who has the right to speak on certain issues. This exclusionary approach can further marginalize already vulnerable voices within the movement.

To address the authenticity paradox, it is crucial to embrace the fluidity and complexity of identities and experiences. Recognizing that authenticity is not fixed but ever-evolving allows for a more inclusive and intersectional understanding of social justice advocacy.

Authenticity should not be seen as an individual pursuit at the expense of collective struggle. The quest for authenticity can be empowering when it aligns with the collective fight against oppression. Striking a balance between individual expression and the larger social justice goals is essential to avoid falling into the authenticity paradox.

Inclusive authenticity recognizes that there is no single authentic experience within a community. It celebrates diverse identities and experiences, rejecting rigid notions of what it means to be "authentic." Embracing inclusive authenticity allows for greater solidarity and coalition-building among various social justice movements.

In navigating the authenticity paradox, social justice advocates must be mindful of the complexities and nuances of identity and representation. By embracing inclusivity, fluidity, and collective empowerment, we can harness the transformative power of authenticity while avoiding the pitfalls of essentialism and exclusion. The quest for authenticity remains central to the struggle for justice, but its true potential can only be realized through an intersectional and empathetic approach.

### Embracing Personal Narratives

Amidst the complexities of the authenticity paradox, embracing personal narratives becomes a powerful tool for reclaiming agency and challenging dominant narratives. Personal narratives are individual stories that provide insight into the lived experiences of individuals within marginalized communities. By amplifying these narratives, social justice movements can create spaces for diverse voices and foster a deeper understanding of the systemic inequalities they face.

Personal narratives have the capacity to empower individuals within marginalized communities. By sharing their stories, individuals can break the silence imposed by oppressive systems and take control of their own narratives. This act of storytelling becomes an act of resistance against erasure and marginalization.

In the face of systemic dehumanization and discrimination, personal narratives humanize the experiences of marginalized individuals. These stories provide a window into the emotions, struggles, and triumphs of real people, challenging the dehumanizing rhetoric that perpetuates structural racism and inequality.

Embracing personal narratives has the potential to shift perspectives and challenge implicit biases. Hearing firsthand accounts of discrimination and injustice compels individuals to confront their own privilege and biases, fostering empathy and understanding across diverse communities.

Personal narratives also highlight the intersectionality of identity and the ways in which multiple forms of oppression intersect. They offer a nuanced understanding of how race, gender, sexuality, disability, and other identities shape an individual's experiences. Recognizing intersectionality within personal narratives deepens the discourse on social justice and fosters greater solidarity.

Personal narratives must be presented with care and respect, avoiding tokenism and exploitation in social justice advocacy. Elevating personal stories solely for performative purposes can further marginalize individuals. True authenticity lies in giving agency to storytellers and acknowledging the diversity of experiences within a community.

Embracing personal narratives also opens the door to building connections and coalitions among various social justice movements. By recognizing the common threads in personal struggles, different communities can find common ground and work together towards collective liberation.

Personal narratives offer a path towards empowerment, understanding, and collective action in the quest for authenticity. Embracing these stories enables social justice movements to center the experiences of marginalized individuals and create a more inclusive and empathetic society. As personal narratives weave together a tapestry of diverse voices, they become a powerful force for transformative change.

## Moving Beyond Performative Activism

As the call for authenticity resonates within social justice movements, there arises a pressing need to move beyond performative activism. Performative activism refers to superficial or symbolic actions that are devoid of substantive impact. While such actions may appear to align with social justice values, they often serve to uphold the status quo rather than challenging it.

Performative activism can be deceptive, giving the illusion of progress while little is done to address the root causes of inequality. In some cases, it may even distract from meaningful change by offering a convenient outlet for superficial gestures.

Social media plays a significant role in the proliferation of performative activism. The ease of sharing images, slogans, and hashtags can lead to a superficial engagement with social justice issues, reducing complex struggles to mere trends.

Corporations and individuals alike have been quick to capitalize on the language of social justice without fully committing to substantive change. Brands may adopt slogans and symbols associated with social justice movements to boost their image without actively dismantling oppressive practices.

To move beyond performative activism, a critical shift towards authentic action is necessary. This requires a commitment to meaningful change, both individually and institutionally.

Authentic action acknowledges the intersectionality of social justice issues and engages with the specific contexts of different communities. It demands an understanding of the unique challenges faced by marginalized groups and a commitment to solidarity.

Authentic action goes beyond cosmetic changes and confronts the power structures that perpetuate inequality. This involves advocating for policy reforms, corporate accountability, and institutional change.

Moving beyond performative activism necessitates holding ourselves and others accountable for our actions. Acknowledging mistakes and learning from them is essential in the pursuit of genuine progress.

True authenticity involves centering the voices and experiences of marginalized communities. It means actively listening and amplifying the stories of those most affected by systemic oppression.

Authentic action entails building sustainable social justice movements that go beyond momentary outrage. It involves organizing, coalition-building, and engaging in long-term advocacy for enduring change.

When moving beyond performative activism, we recognize that the struggle for social justice demands more than surface-level gestures. It requires a profound commitment to authenticity, empathy, and tangible action. By embracing authenticity in our activism, we can build a more just and equitable world for all.

## The Intersection of Culture and Activism

The critical role of the intersection of culture and activism becomes evident in the pursuit of authenticity within social justice movements. Culture, with its rich tapestry of traditions, art, language, and collective memory, shapes the way individuals perceive and respond to social issues. Recognizing this intersection offers a deeper understanding of the unique challenges faced by diverse communities and the power of cultural expression in driving social change.

For marginalized communities, cultural identity serves as a source of empowerment and resilience. Embracing one's cultural heritage can be an act of resistance against assimilation and erasure. Activism that values and celebrates cultural identity allows individuals to assert their agency and reclaim their narratives.

Cultural activism refers to the use of cultural expressions, such as music, art, dance, and storytelling, as tools for social change. These forms of expression have the potential to transcend linguistic and geographical barriers, creating connections and solidarity across diverse communities.

Understanding the cultural nuances of the communities being served is essential for effective activism. Cultural competence requires sensitivity and awareness of the histories, traditions, and values that shape the experiences of those involved in the movement.

The intersectionality of culture and identity underscores the diversity within social justice movements. Different cultural contexts can shape the experiences and priorities of individuals within a movement. Acknowledging these differences fosters more inclusive and effective activism.

While cultural exchange can promote understanding and appreciation, cultural appropriation is an exploitative act that commodifies and distorts cultural symbols without respect for their origin or significance. Authentic activism respects the boundaries between exchange and Artistic expression can be a powerful form of activism. Art has the ability to challenge norms, provoke emotions, and inspire action. From protest songs to street murals, art serves as a medium through which activists can communicate their messages to the broader public.

Language shapes the discourse surrounding social justice issues. Authentic activism demands the use of inclusive and respectful language that acknowledges the diversity of experiences and identities.

Cultural hegemony, where dominant cultural norms perpetuate inequality, can pose challenges for cultural activism. Overcoming these challenges requires disrupting entrenched power dynamics and centering marginalized voices.

The intersection of culture and activism offers a path towards more authentic and transformative social justice movements. By recognizing the power of cultural identity and expression, activists can build bridges of understanding and empathy, fostering solidarity among diverse communities in the pursuit of a more just and equitable world.

## Navigating Allyship with Authenticity

As social justice movements call for allyship, the quest for authenticity becomes paramount. Allyship involves individuals from privileged groups supporting marginalized communities in their struggle for justice. However, the act of allyship can easily slip into performative gestures if not approached with genuine authenticity.

Authentic allyship begins with an honest examination of one's own privilege and power within society. Recognizing the advantages one holds and how these advantages intersect with systems of oppression is essential for authentic allyship.

Authentic allyship requires centering the voices and experiences of the marginalized communities being supported. Allies must actively listen, learn, and amplify these voices, rather than speaking over or for them.

Performative allyship often involves a "savior" complex, where allies seek validation or praise for their actions. Authentic allies understand that they are not "saving" anyone but rather working in solidarity to dismantle oppressive systems.

Authentic allies are not passive bystanders. They actively advocate for change and support the demands of marginalized communities. This may involve showing up at protests, engaging in direct action, or using one's influence to effect systemic change.

Authentic allies are open to critique and are willing to reflect on their actions and biases. When mistakes are made, they take responsibility and commit to learning and growing from them.

Allyship is not a one-time act but an ongoing commitment to unlearning oppressive behaviors and supporting social justice efforts.

Authentic allies understand that true change requires dedication and perseverance.

Authentic allyship acknowledges the intersections of identities and experiences within social justice movements. It understands that different marginalized communities face unique struggles and that solidarity must be intersectional.

Authentic allies understand that they cannot fully understand the experiences of those they support. They recognize the importance of respecting boundaries and not imposing their own solutions or narratives onto marginalized communities.

Authentic allies use their platforms and privilege to amplify the voices of the marginalized, rather than appropriating their stories or experiences for personal gain.

Navigating allyship with authenticity requires humility, empathy, and a commitment to ongoing learning. By recognizing their position within systems of privilege and power, authentic allies work in solidarity with marginalized communities to create lasting and transformative change.

## The Impact of Authentic Leadership

Authentic leadership within social justice movements can have a profound impact on the effectiveness and sustainability of those movements. When leaders exemplify authenticity, they inspire trust, foster genuine connections, and create an environment where individuals feel empowered to contribute their unique strengths and perspectives.

Authentic leaders prioritize honesty and transparency, building trust with their followers. By openly acknowledging challenges, admitting mistakes, and being consistent in their values and actions, these leaders establish credibility within the movement.

Authentic leaders foster a culture of collaboration, valuing the input of all individuals within the movement. They actively seek diverse perspectives and encourage inclusivity, recognizing that the strength of the movement lies in its diversity.

Leaders who lead with authenticity ignite passion and commitment in their followers. By sharing their personal stories, vulnerabilities, and deep commitment to the cause, they create an emotional connection that motivates others to take action.

Authentic leaders empower their followers by acknowledging their agency and expertise. They create opportunities for individuals to take on leadership roles and contribute meaningfully to the movement's goals.

Authentic leaders are better equipped to navigate challenges and setbacks. Their honesty and transparency help the movement weather criticism and maintain its focus on its core values.

Leaders who prioritize authenticity create a sense of belonging within the movement. They foster a community where individuals feel seen, heard, and valued, reinforcing their commitment to the cause.

Authentic leaders model a commitment to continuous learning and growth. They openly reflect on their own biases and privilege, demonstrating vulnerability and encouraging others to do the same.

When leaders value authenticity, they prioritize self-care and well-being within the movement. By acknowledging the toll of social justice work, they encourage individuals to take breaks, seek support, and prevent burnout.

The impact of authentic leadership extends beyond the immediate followers. Authentic leaders inspire and cultivate new leaders within the movement, creating a positive ripple effect that can shape the movement's trajectory for years to come.

By embracing authenticity, leaders can elevate the effectiveness of social justice movements, creating spaces where individuals are empowered to bring their whole selves to the cause. The impact of authentic leadership extends far beyond the leader's role, fostering a culture of trust, collaboration, and genuine connection within the movement.

## Fostering Inclusive Spaces

Inclusive spaces are vital for the success and impact of social justice movements. When authenticity is at the core of these spaces, they become environments where individuals from diverse backgrounds feel welcome, heard, and empowered to contribute fully.

Authentic inclusive spaces acknowledge the intersectionality of identities and experiences. They recognize that individuals navigate multiple forms of oppression and privilege, and ensure that the movement addresses the unique challenges faced by different communities.

Inclusive spaces challenge dominant narratives that perpetuate stereotypes and inequalities. They create platforms for marginalized voices to share their stories, challenging oppressive narratives and empowering individuals to reclaim their own narratives.

Authentic inclusive spaces prioritize intersectional leadership, ensuring that individuals from marginalized communities are represented in leadership positions. This practice enables diverse perspectives to influence decision-making and strategy.

Inclusive spaces foster a culture of active listening and empathy. Participants are encouraged to listen deeply to one another's experiences, validating each other's emotions and struggles.

Authentic inclusive spaces are not afraid of difficult conversations. They encourage open dialogue about privilege, bias, and systemic barriers, fostering a collective commitment to unlearning and growth. Inclusive spaces actively cultivate allyship and solidarity among members. They provide resources and support to individuals seeking to become effective allies to marginalized communities.

Events, workshops, and programming in inclusive spaces are intersectional and responsive to the needs and interests of diverse participants. They avoid tokenizing and represent the multifaceted realities of the movement's members.

Authentic inclusive spaces prioritize the recognition and addressing of microaggressions. They provide resources and education to help individuals understand the impact of their words and actions on others.

Inclusive spaces recognize the need for healing and provide support for individuals who have experienced trauma or discrimination. They prioritize self-care and mental well-being within the movement.

Inclusive spaces are committed to accountability and learning. They hold members responsible for their actions and support them in their journey towards greater understanding and allyship.

Fostering inclusive spaces is essential for building a truly transformative social justice movement. By centering intersectionality, challenging dominant narratives, and actively supporting diverse voices, these spaces become catalysts for meaningful change and collective empowerment. The quest for authenticity within inclusive spaces leads to a movement that is more reflective, responsive, and capable of dismantling oppressive systems.

## Intersectionality as an Authentic Framework

Amidst the quest for authenticity, social justice movements are increasingly embracing intersectionality as a guiding framework. Coined by Kimberlé Crenshaw, intersectionality recognizes that individuals' experiences of oppression and privilege are shaped by the intersection of various social identities, such as race, gender, sexuality, class, disability, and more. Understanding and incorporating intersectionality into the movement's ethos and practices is crucial for fostering genuine inclusivity and equity.

Intersectionality as an authentic framework acknowledges the complex and multifaceted nature of people's lives. It recognizes that no individual's experiences can be reduced to a single identity and that oppression and privilege are interconnected and interwoven.

Authentic intersectionality challenges the limitations of single-issue activism. It encourages the movement to embrace a broader and more nuanced approach to social justice that considers the overlapping and interlocking systems of oppression.

Intersectionality prioritizes amplifying the voices of marginalized communities, centering their experiences, and acknowledging their expertise in shaping solutions to the issues they face.

An authentic intersectional framework fosters solidarity among diverse groups, recognizing that the fight for justice is interconnected. It encourages individuals from different communities to come together, share experiences, and support one another.

Intersectionality requires an in-depth analysis of power structures that perpetuate oppression. By understanding how various identities intersect and are situated within these power structures, the movement gains a more comprehensive understanding of social inequality.

An authentic approach to intersectionality calls on individuals to recognize their privilege and how it impacts their perceptions and actions. It emphasizes the importance of leveraging privilege to challenge systemic injustices.

Intersectionality acknowledges that tensions and hierarchies can exist within marginalized communities. An authentic framework actively seeks to address these issues and build bridges across differences.

Authentic intersectionality extends to policy and advocacy work, recognizing that effective solutions must consider the intersecting needs of different communities.

An authentic intersectional approach critiques tokenism and superficial diversity efforts. It encourages meaningful representation and engagement of marginalized communities.

Intersectionality, when embraced authentically, has the transformative potential to reshape the movement's priorities, strategies, and vision. By acknowledging the interplay of identities and experiences, the movement becomes more resilient, adaptable, and effective in dismantling oppressive systems.

Centering intersectionality as an authentic framework in the quest for social justice ensures that the movement is rooted in genuine understanding, empathy, and solidarity. It is a powerful tool for fostering inclusivity, empowerment, and collective action towards a more equitable and just society.

## Maintaining Authenticity in the Digital Age

As social justice movements navigate the digital landscape, maintaining authenticity becomes both critical and challenging. The Digital Age offers unprecedented opportunities for connecting with a global audience, mobilizing supporters, and amplifying marginalized voices. However, it also presents risks of performative activism, misrepresentation, and co-optation. To uphold authenticity in the digital realm, the movement must be mindful of its actions and strategies.

Social media platforms have revolutionized the way social justice movements communicate and organize. They offer accessible channels for grassroots activism, enabling individuals from diverse backgrounds to share their stories and mobilize support.

Amidst the digital era, the potency of authentic storytelling endures as an influential instrument to convey the lived experiences of marginalized communities. Genuine narratives resonate with audiences, fostering empathy and understanding.

The digital space can inadvertently promote performative activism, where actions are superficial and lack meaningful impact. The movement must be vigilant in distinguishing genuine advocacy from mere virtue signaling.

Maintaining authenticity requires transparency and accountability in the movement's actions and decision-making processes. Openly acknowledging mistakes and learning from them fosters trust with supporters.

The Digital Age has also given rise to cancel culture, where individuals are swiftly judged and ostracized for their perceived missteps. An authentic approach seeks to challenge cancel culture, emphasizing education and growth over punishment.

Misinformation and disinformation pose significant challenges to maintaining authenticity. The movement must be diligent in fact-checking and sharing accurate information to preserve credibility.

As the movement adopts technology for its advocacy, ethical considerations must guide its usage. Safeguarding privacy and data security are essential to protect activists and marginalized communities.

Authenticity in the digital age demands inclusive digital spaces that prioritize marginalized voices and foster respectful dialogue. Moderation and community guidelines are essential to maintain safe environments.

While digital platforms provide global reach, authentic activism must also empower grassroots movements at the local level. It ensures that change is driven by the affected communities themselves.

An authentic approach finds a balance between online and offline activism, recognizing the importance of real-world organizing and advocacy alongside digital engagement.

Maintaining authenticity in the digital age necessitates meaningful impact measurement. The movement should focus on tangible outcomes and progress, rather than solely on metrics like social media followers.

By understanding and actively navigating the opportunities and challenges of the Digital Age, social justice movements can maintain their authenticity and continue their essential work of fighting for justice and equality. Embracing technology while remaining true to the movement's core values strengthens the quest for a more equitable and inclusive world.

The quest for authenticity within social justice movements is a multifaceted and dynamic journey. It demands a genuine commitment to equity, justice, and inclusivity. Throughout this chapter, we explored the challenges and opportunities that arise when seeking authenticity in activism. We delved into the importance of embracing personal narratives, moving beyond performative activism, and understanding the intersection of culture and activism. We also explored the significance of intersectionality as an authentic framework and the need to foster inclusive spaces. Moreover, we highlighted the impact of authentic leadership, particularly in inspiring others to join the cause and championing social change.

As we navigate the complex landscape of social justice, maintaining authenticity becomes increasingly crucial. Authenticity acts as the cornerstone of trust, unity, and collaboration within movements. It empowers individuals to stand firm in their convictions while also being open to dialogue and growth. Authenticity bridges the gap between lived experiences and shared values, forming connections that transcend boundaries of race, class, gender, and geography.

However, the pursuit of authenticity does not come without challenges. The rise of performative activism, the weaponization of "woke," and the co-optation of movements by corporate interests create formidable obstacles. In the digital age, maintaining authenticity becomes even more critical, as social media platforms amplify both genuine advocacy and superficial gestures.

To overcome these challenges, social justice movements must foster a culture of authenticity. This involves embracing diverse voices, promoting transparency, and encouraging self-reflection. Authenticity requires humility, acknowledging that we are all constantly learning and evolving in our understanding of social issues.

It is essential to recognize that authenticity is not a fixed destination but an ongoing process. It is a commitment to remain true to the core principles of justice, empathy, and respect for the dignity of all individuals. Authenticity calls for engaging in the difficult conversations, holding ourselves accountable, and amplifying the voices of those who have historically been marginalized.

The quest for authenticity is fundamental to the success and longevity of social justice movements. It is an ongoing journey that requires collective dedication, self-awareness, and a willingness to evolve. By remaining authentic in our pursuit of a more equitable world, we can forge transformative change and build a society that honors the inherent worth and dignity of every human being.

*"Listen, they lack true originality and have now co-opted a term that*
*has distorted dialogue, proliferated viral ignorance and marginalized a nuanced discussion"*

# CHAPTER 8
# CHALLENGING THE
# CONSERVATIVE MISAPPROPRIATION

The term "woke" has evolved from its roots as a call for social awareness and activism to a contentious battlefield in the cultural and political landscape. Unfortunately, it has also been appropriated and
weaponized by some elements of the conservative movement. In this
chapter, we explore how the word "woke" has been misappropriated
by the conservative party and how this has had a detrimental impact on social justice movements. We explore the ramifications of this
misappropriation on public discourse and its impact on endeavors to
combat systemic racism and inequality.

The misappropriation of "woke" by the conservative party is a prime
example of linguistic and cultural hijacking. What was once a term
synonymous with being conscious of social injustices and advocating
for positive change has been twisted into a pejorative. It is used to

disparage social justice advocates and label their efforts as misguided, radical, or even dangerous.

The conservative misappropriation of "woke" aims to discredit the legitimate concerns raised by those fighting for equity, diversity, and inclusion. By distorting the meaning of the term, some factions of the conservative party seek to undermine the credibility of progressive movements and portray them as divisive or even anti-American. This deliberate misrepresentation has had a polarizing effect on public opinion, inhibiting constructive dialogue on crucial social issues.

Moreover, the misappropriation of "woke" is a strategic maneuver to shift focus away from the very real structural racism and systemic inequalities that persist in our society. It allows the conservative party to divert attention from its own complicity in upholding oppressive systems and policies, positioning themselves as champions of traditional values and national identity.

However, we must not allow the misappropriation of "woke" to silence our advocacy for a more just and equitable world. Challenging the conservative misappropriation requires understanding the tactics used to co-opt the term and developing strategies to reclaim its true meaning. By engaging in thoughtful and informed discussions, we can counter the misleading narratives and create space for authentic dialogue.

We will explore the historical and ideological context behind the conservative misappropriation of "woke." We will also analyze the impact of this misappropriation on public perception and the broader implications for social justice movements. By understanding the tactics employed to distort the meaning of "woke," we can better navigate the complex landscape of modern activism and work towards dismantling the structures of oppression that persist in our society.

## The Origins of the Misappropriation

The misappropriation of "woke" by the conservative party did not occur in isolation. It is rooted in a broader ideological struggle over the narratives surrounding social justice and progressive movements. To understand its origins, we must delve into the historical and political context that gave rise to this misrepresentation.

In the early 2010s, "woke" gained popularity within social justice circles as a term to describe heightened awareness of systemic injustices and a commitment to activism. It was a call to action for individuals to be mindful of the deep-rooted inequalities that permeate society and to actively work towards dismantling them. As the term gained traction, it also drew criticism from conservative circles that viewed it as emblematic of a progressive agenda that threatened traditional values.

As the conservative movement grappled with the growing influence of progressive ideals, it sought to discredit and delegitimize the language used by social justice advocates. The misappropriation of "woke" became a strategic tool to achieve this goal. By framing "woke" as a radical and divisive ideology, the conservative party could rally its base around a narrative of preserving traditional values and resisting what they perceived as a dangerous left-wing agenda.

Conservative media outlets played a crucial role in propagating the misappropriation of "woke." Through opinion pieces, talk shows, and social media campaigns, the term was repeatedly associated with identity politics and political correctness. This framing effectively transformed "woke" from a term of empowerment to a symbol of ideological excess, blurring the lines between genuine social justice efforts and exaggerated caricatures of activism.

Furthermore, the conservative misappropriation of "woke" took advantage of the complexities of language and culture. The term's roots in African American vernacular and its association with progressive social movements made it vulnerable to manipulation. By labeling "woke" as a radical leftist ideology, the conservative party could tap into pre-existing fears and biases among their audience, fostering a sense of moral outrage and cultural resistance.

Ultimately, the misappropriation of "woke" allowed the conservative movement to create a false binary between being "woke" and being patriotic, effectively painting social justice advocates as unpatriotic and anti-American. This binary perpetuates a divisive "us versus them" narrative that hampers genuine dialogue and progress towards a more inclusive society.

Next, we will examine how the conservative misappropriation of "woke" intersects with broader issues of identity politics and polarized public discourse. By understanding the origins of this misappropriation, we can begin to unravel its impact on public perception and work towards reclaiming the true spirit of "woke" as a call for justice and equality.

## "Wokeness" as a Cultural Battleground

The misappropriation of "woke" by the conservative party has turned it into a cultural battleground, where ideas of identity, justice, and social progress clash. This battleground is marked by a fierce struggle over the meaning and representation of "woke" and its association with broader issues of culture and values.

Conservatives have used "wokeness" as a lightning rod to rally their base and mobilize public opinion against progressive social movements. They argue that the excessive focus on identity and political correctness stifles free speech and undermines traditional values. This framing has led to a perception that "wokeness" threatens the very fabric of society and seeks to erase cherished cultural norms.

On the other side, social justice advocates view "woke" as a necessary tool for challenging systemic inequalities and promoting social change. They argue that the conservative misappropriation of "woke" is a deliberate attempt to delegitimize their struggle for justice and equality. To them, the conservative backlash against "wokeness" is a defense of privilege and a refusal to acknowledge the realities of structural racism and other forms of oppression.

The misappropriation of "woke" has also created divisions within communities and institutions. It has become a polarizing term, with some embracing it as a symbol of progressivism, while others reject it as a threat to their cultural identity. This polarization has further exacerbated tensions in an already divided society, making it challenging to find common ground and foster genuine dialogue.

In this cultural battleground, there is a danger of losing sight of the original intent of "woke" as a call for social justice and equality. Both sides tend to engage in rhetoric that oversimplifies and misrepresents the other, hindering meaningful discussions about the pressing issues facing society.

To move beyond this impasse, it is crucial to recognize the complexity of "wokeness" and the diverse perspectives surrounding it. Rather than allowing it to be a divisive tool, we must reclaim "woke" as a term that unites individuals in their commitment to addressing social injustices. This requires acknowledging the legitimacy of different viewpoints and engaging in constructive conversations that bridge ideological divides.

By embracing an approach that centers on empathy, understanding, and a commitment to justice, we can begin to challenge the conservative misappropriation of "woke" and pave the way for a more inclusive and equitable society. In the following sections, we will explore ways to navigate this cultural battleground and foster a more constructive and authentic discourse around "wokeness."

## The Weaponization of "Woke" Against Progressivism

The conservative misappropriation of "woke" has not only led to a distortion of its original meaning but also resulted in the weaponization of the term against progressivism and social justice movements. By turning "wokeness" into a pejorative, conservatives have sought to undermine the legitimacy of progressive causes and discredit those advocating for change.

Conservative media outlets and political figures have strategically deployed the term "woke" to demonize progressive activists and dismiss their concerns. They accuse "woke" activists of promoting a divisive agenda that seeks to undermine American values and traditions. This weaponization has been especially effective in mobilizing conservative voters and creating a sense of threat and urgency around the perceived dangers of progressivism.

One of the key strategies in the weaponization of "woke" is the mischaracterization of social justice movements as inherently radical and extreme. By focusing on isolated incidents or outliers, conservatives paint a misleading picture of the entire movement, allowing them to dismiss legitimate calls for justice and equality as mere instances of "cancel culture" or political correctness gone awry.

Moreover, conservatives often claim that "wokeness" stifles free speech and promotes censorship, using this argument to push back against progressive activism and justify their own actions. This tactic has been particularly potent in debates around academic freedom and the role of universities in promoting diversity and inclusion.

The weaponization of "woke" has also seeped into corporate and public institutions. Fearful of backlash and reputational damage, some organizations have shied away from supporting progressive causes or engaging in authentic allyship, opting instead for performative gestures of support. This has further fueled the misrepresentation of "wokeness" as a superficial and divisive ideology.

To challenge the weaponization of "woke," it is essential to engage in nuanced and evidence-based discussions about the goals and methods of social justice movements. Rather than falling into the trap of polarized rhetoric, it is crucial to highlight the positive impacts of progressive activism and the tangible changes it has brought to society.

Additionally, emphasizing the interconnectedness of different social justice movements and the shared pursuit of a more equitable world can help counter the narrative that "wokeness" is inherently divisive. By showcasing the power of solidarity and collective action, we can challenge the conservative misappropriation of "woke" and demonstrate its potential as a force for positive change.

## The "Woke" as a Divisive Tool

The misappropriation of "woke" by the conservative movement has also served as a divisive tool in the political landscape. By framing "wokeness" as a threat to the fabric of society, conservatives have sought to create a sense of "us versus them," pitting different groups against each other based on their views on social justice issues.

Conservatives have used the term "woke" to mobilize their base and rally support around a shared opposition to progressive ideas. They have portrayed themselves as defenders of traditional values and guardians of a supposedly under attack American identity. This strategy aims to appeal to a sense of nostalgia for a perceived simpler and more homogenous past.

In the context of identity politics, the misappropriation of "woke" has exacerbated existing divisions along racial, gender, and cultural lines. It has been wielded to dismiss the grievances of marginalized communities and maintain the status quo, reinforcing the power dynamics that perpetuate systemic inequities.

Furthermore, the weaponization of "woke" has led to a polarization in public discourse, hindering meaningful dialogue and cooperation between different ideological groups. By demonizing "wokeness" and characterizing it as an existential threat, conservatives have made it challenging to find common ground on issues of social justice and equality.

The divisive nature of the misappropriation of "woke" is evident in the media landscape, where pundits and commentators often use the term to create sensationalized narratives that play on fears and prejudices. This sensationalism fuels the perception that "wokeness" is a radical ideology at odds with mainstream values, even though its core principles revolve around justice and inclusivity.

To challenge the divisive use of "woke," it is crucial to engage in nuanced discussions that emphasize the shared values and aspirations that unite different groups. By focusing on common goals, such as equality, fairness, and human rights, it is possible to bridge divides and foster empathy across ideological lines.

Moreover, reframing "wokeness" as a movement that seeks to uplift the voices of marginalized communities and challenge systemic injustices can help counter the divisive narrative propagated by the conservative misappropriation. Emphasizing the potential for positive change and collective progress can create space for constructive dialogue and bridge-building in pursuit of a more equitable society. By reclaiming the authentic essence of "woke," we can work towards a more inclusive and united future.

### The "Woke" Backlash: Resistance and Responses

The conservative misappropriation of "woke" has not gone uncontested. As the term became more widely used as a pejorative, a backlash from progressives and social justice advocates emerged, pushing back against the distorted narrative and defending the original meaning and intent of "wokeness."

One of the primary responses to the "woke" backlash has been a focus on education and awareness. Social justice activists and organizations have sought to clarify the true meaning of "wokeness" and its historical roots, emphasizing its connection to the pursuit of equality and justice. This educational effort aims to debunk the caricature created by conservatives and provide a more accurate understanding of the term.

In addition to education, many activists have engaged in reclaiming "wokeness" by amplifying the voices of marginalized communities and centering their experiences. By highlighting the lived realities of those affected by systemic oppression, activists challenge the misappropriation and show that "wokeness" is not an abstract ideology but a response to real-world injustices.

Progressives have also sought to counter the divisive tactics employed by the conservative misappropriation by emphasizing the importance of solidarity and coalition-building. Instead of allowing "wokeness" to be used as a wedge to divide different communities, activists have worked to find common ground and build bridges between various social justice movements.

Furthermore, individuals and organizations have pushed for systemic change, advocating for policies that address the root causes of inequality and dismantling oppressive structures. By focusing on concrete actions and tangible outcomes, activists challenge the notion that "wokeness" is merely performative and ineffective.

The "woke" backlash has also spurred conversations within progressive circles about the need for self-reflection and growth. Some have critiqued aspects of the social justice movement and called for a more nuanced and inclusive approach that recognizes the diversity of perspectives within the movement itself.

Ultimately, the resistance to the conservative misappropriation of "woke" is an ongoing process that requires ongoing engagement, dialogue, and collective action. By challenging the false narratives and divisive tactics used by conservatives, activists and advocates can work towards reclaiming the authentic meaning of "wokeness" and advancing the cause of social justice and equality.

### Authenticity and the Fight Against Misappropriation

Amid the battle over the meaning of "wokeness," authenticity has emerged as a powerful tool in the fight against its misappropriation. As progressives seek to reclaim the term and its original intent, they emphasize the importance of staying true to the principles of social justice and equality.

Authenticity in this context refers to a commitment to genuine values and actions that align with the pursuit of justice. It involves being transparent about intentions and motivations and avoiding performative gestures or empty signifiers. By centering authenticity, progressives aim to distinguish their advocacy from the superficial co-optation attempted by conservative forces.

One of the key elements in the fight against misappropriation is acknowledging and addressing the valid concerns raised by critics. Rather than dismissing all critiques as attacks, social justice advocates embrace self-reflection and are open to constructive feedback. This commitment to growth and learning allows for a more authentic and effective movement that continually evolves to meet the challenges of advancing social change.

Another aspect of authenticity is the rejection of divisive tactics and a commitment to building bridges and finding common ground. While the conservative misappropriation has sought to use "wokeness" as a way to sow discord, progressives emphasize the need for solidarity and unity among different social justice movements. This authentic approach recognizes that true progress is achieved when marginalized communities work together to dismantle intersecting systems of oppression.

The fight against misappropriation also requires a recognition of the power dynamics at play. Authentic advocacy involves amplifying the voices of those most impacted by injustice and deferring to their expertise and leadership. It resists the urge to co-opt or dominate movements and instead centers the experiences and needs of the communities affected.

Lastly, an authentic response to misappropriation demands consistency and commitment. It requires staying true to the principles of justice and equality, even in the face of opposition or adversity. By holding fast to their values, social justice advocates can counter attempts to dilute or distort the meaning of "wokeness" and maintain the integrity of the movement.

The fight against the conservative misappropriation of "wokeness" relies on authenticity as a guiding principle. By remaining true to their values, embracing self-reflection, building solidarity, amplifying marginalized voices, and demonstrating consistency, progressives can effectively challenge the distortion of "wokeness" and reclaim its true meaning in the pursuit of a more just and equitable society.

## Engaging in Constructive Dialogue

In the face of the conservative misappropriation of "wokeness," engaging in constructive dialogue becomes crucial for advancing meaningful discourse and countering divisive tactics. While the misappropriation seeks to weaponize "wokeness" for political gain, constructive dialogue allows for a more nuanced understanding of the complexities surrounding social justice issues.

One of the key components of constructive dialogue is active listening. Rather than engaging in a monologue of opposing viewpoints, participants must genuinely listen to each other's perspectives. Active listening involves empathy and a willingness to understand the concerns and experiences of others, even if they differ from one's own. By creating a space for genuine understanding, constructive dialogue can bridge ideological divides and foster a more collaborative approach to addressing societal challenges.

Another aspect of constructive dialogue is the recognition that language matters. The misuse of terms like "wokeness" by conservatives has led to confusion and polarization. Engaging in dialogue requires clarifying definitions and avoiding jargon that may alienate or misrepresent the intentions of social justice advocates. By using language that is inclusive and accessible, participants can establish common ground for discussion.

Constructive dialogue also involves acknowledging the complexity of social issues. The misappropriation of "wokeness" often oversimplifies complex problems to fit into partisan narratives. Instead, engaging in honest and informed conversations about the root causes of social inequities allows for a more comprehensive understanding of the challenges at hand. By delving into the historical and structural factors contributing to systemic oppression, participants can develop more effective strategies for change.

Furthermore, constructive dialogue emphasizes the importance of finding shared values and goals. While there may be disagreements on specific approaches or policies, identifying common ground can lead to collaborative efforts that transcend partisan divisions. By focusing on shared aspirations for a just and equitable society, participants can move beyond performative debates and work towards tangible solutions.

Lastly, engaging in constructive dialogue requires a commitment to respectful discourse. In the face of heated political rhetoric, maintaining a respectful and civil tone is essential for fostering a productive exchange of ideas. This approach not only helps to build trust among participants but also encourages others to join the conversation.

Constructive dialogue is a powerful tool for challenging the conservative misappropriation of "wokeness" and advancing meaningful conversations about social justice. By actively listening, using inclusive language, acknowledging complexity, finding common ground, and maintaining respect, participants can contribute to a more authentic and constructive dialogue that seeks to address the root causes of inequality and create positive change in society.

### Amplifying Marginalized Voices

In the fight against the conservative misappropriation of "wokeness," amplifying marginalized voices becomes a critical strategy to counter the dominant narratives and bring attention to the authentic experiences of those most impacted by social injustices. Centering the voices of marginalized communities provides a more accurate and nuanced understanding of the challenges they face, and it is essential in dismantling the distorted misappropriation propagated by conservatives.

One of the primary ways to amplify marginalized voices is through storytelling. Narratives have the power to humanize and contextualize complex issues. Sharing personal stories and experiences allows marginalized individuals to reclaim their agency and challenge the stereotypes perpetuated by the misappropriation. By providing a platform for their narratives, their struggles, resilience, and contributions to society are brought to the forefront, shifting the focus away from divisive mischaracterizations.

Social media and digital platforms play a significant role in amplifying marginalized voices. Online spaces enable individuals to share their stories, perspectives, and insights with a global audience. Hashtags, online campaigns, and viral content can rapidly amplify the experiences of marginalized communities, raising awareness and demanding accountability from those in positions of power.

Furthermore, uplifting underrepresented voices in mainstream media and public forums is crucial. Media outlets have a responsibility to provide a platform for diverse perspectives, challenging the narratives perpetuated by the conservative misappropriation. By featuring diverse voices in news, entertainment, and opinion pieces, media can help dismantle the distorted portrayal of "wokeness" and promote a more accurate representation of social justice issues.

Another way to amplify marginalized voices is through allyship and coalition-building. Allies, who are individuals with privilege, can use their platforms and influence to elevate and support marginalized communities. By actively listening to and standing in solidarity with these communities, allies can help bring attention to the misappropriation and advocate for a more equitable society.

Educational institutions and organizations also play a significant role in amplifying marginalized voices. Incorporating diverse perspectives and experiences into curricula and programming challenges the dominant narrative and fosters a more inclusive learning environment. Additionally, encouraging dialogue and understanding among students from various backgrounds promotes empathy and dismantles stereotypes.

Amplifying marginalized voices is a powerful and necessary response to the conservative misappropriation of "wokeness." Through storytelling, social media, mainstream media, allyship, and educational efforts, marginalized communities can reclaim their narratives and challenge the divisive misrepresentations. By centering their experiences, we can work towards a more authentic understanding of social justice issues and strive for a society that values and uplifts the voices of all its members.

## The Responsibility of Media and Information Sharing

In the battle against the conservative misappropriation of "wokeness," media and information sharing platforms hold a significant responsibility in shaping public perceptions and promoting authentic discourse. The media's role in disseminating information and framing narratives can either perpetuate the misappropriation or be a powerful force in challenging it.

One of the primary responsibilities of media outlets is to adhere to journalistic integrity and fact-checking practices. By ensuring that news stories and reports are accurate, unbiased, and based on credible sources, media organizations can counter the spread of misinformation and misrepresentation perpetuated by conservative forces. Fact-based reporting fosters a more informed and nuanced understanding of social justice issues and dismantles the divisive narratives propagated by the misappropriation.

Furthermore, media outlets must strive to represent diverse perspectives authentically. Centering marginalized voices and experiences in news stories, opinion pieces, and documentaries helps challenge the misappropriation by providing a more comprehensive and accurate portrayal of social justice issues. This inclusivity also fosters a sense of belonging and representation for underrepresented communities, promoting a more equitable society.

Social media platforms and information-sharing websites also have a role in combating the misappropriation. They must prioritize content moderation and fact-checking to prevent the spread of misinformation and disinformation that fuels the misappropriation. These platforms should also be transparent about their content moderation policies to ensure that they are not inadvertently amplifying divisive narratives.

Promoting media literacy and critical thinking skills among the public is another essential aspect of challenging the misappropriation. Education on how to discern credible sources and fact-check information can help individuals navigate the overwhelming amount of content on the internet and social media and identify the manipulative tactics employed by those misappropriating "wokeness" for their own agendas.

Media organizations and information-sharing platforms must also actively work to diversify their workforce. A diverse and inclusive staff brings a broader range of perspectives and insights to the table, resulting in more accurate and authentic reporting. Moreover, promoting diversity in media leadership positions can influence editorial decisions and foster a culture of inclusivity.

The responsibility of media and information sharing in challenging the conservative misappropriation of "wokeness" is immense. Adhering to journalistic integrity, representing diverse perspectives, promoting media literacy, and fostering a diverse workforce are all crucial steps in countering the divisive narratives and misinformation perpetuated by the misappropriation. By fulfilling this responsibility, media and information-sharing platforms can contribute to a more authentic and inclusive public discourse on social justice issues.

The conservative misappropriation of "wokeness" is a multifaceted phenomenon that aims to undermine social justice movements and co-opt progressive ideals for divisive purposes. Throughout this chapter, we have explored the origins and tactics of this misappropriation, its impact on public discourse, and the challenges it presents to authentic activism.

The misappropriation of "wokeness" serves as a political tool for conservatives to vilify and discredit progressive movements. By framing social justice efforts as "woke" and promoting a distorted understanding of these movements, they seek to create a false narrative that pits progressive ideas against conservative values. This misrepresentation can lead to increased polarization and hinder constructive dialogue.

However, challenging this misappropriation requires a concerted effort from various stakeholders. Progressives must reclaim the narrative by staying true to their authentic goals and values. Emphasizing intersectionality, diversity, and inclusivity within social justice movements helps counter the divisive tactics employed by those appropriating "wokeness" for their own gains.

Additionally, amplifying marginalized voices and engaging in constructive dialogue is crucial to combatting the misappropriation. By centering the experiences of those most impacted by social injustices and actively listening to their perspectives, the authenticity of social justice movements becomes evident.

Furthermore, media organizations and information-sharing platforms have a significant responsibility in countering the misappropriation. Fact-based reporting, representation of diverse perspectives, and transparency in content moderation policies can mitigate the spread of misinformation and divisiveness.

Challenging the conservative misappropriation of "wokeness" is an ongoing endeavor that requires vigilance and commitment. Authentic activism, grounded in genuine intentions and inclusive approaches, is essential to maintaining the integrity of social justice movements. By fostering spaces for constructive dialogue and promoting media literacy, we can create a more informed and nuanced public discourse that resists the divisive narratives perpetuated by the misappropriation.

The fight against the conservative misappropriation of "wokeness" is not just a battle of ideologies but also a battle for the authenticity of social justice movements. By staying true to their principles and engaging in constructive dialogue, progressives can reclaim the narrative and navigate a path toward a more inclusive and equitable society. Only by embracing authenticity and centering marginalized voices can we overcome the challenges posed by the misappropriation and work towards meaningful social change.

*"When 'woke' becomes an empty signifier, genuine awareness is replaced by hollow virtue."*

# CHAPTER 9
# THE DANGER OF EMPTY SIGNIFIERS

In present-day discussions, the widespread utilization of empty signifiers has emerged as a prominent obstacle, hindering meaningful communication and impeding social progress. An empty signifier refers to a term, phrase, or symbol that lacks specific meaning or content, yet is evocative and emotionally charged. These signifiers are often used strategically to mobilize people, shape narratives, and influence public opinion. However, their lack of substance can obscure critical issues, stifle genuine dialogue, and even be manipulated for nefarious purposes.

This chapter investigates the dangers posed by empty signifiers, focusing on their manipulation, consequences, and impact on social and political landscapes. By exploring specific examples and examining the mechanisms behind their use, we seek to shed light on the insidious nature of empty signifiers and their implications for society.

Empty signifiers can serve as powerful tools in political and cultural contexts. They are often used to rally supporters around a vague and emotionally charged idea, tapping into deeply held values and beliefs without providing concrete solutions or policy proposals. By harnessing the power of emotions, these signifiers can mobilize a following based on shared sentiments, leading to a highly charged and polarized environment.

Moreover, empty signifiers have been used to hijack social justice movements and co-opt them for alternative agendas. This form of manipulation can dilute the original objectives of such movements and undermine progress towards meaningful change. The misappropriation of terms like "equity" and "diversity" as empty signifiers can detract from the genuine pursuit of social justice and inclusivity.

The consequences of empty signifiers extend beyond politics and activism. In media and advertising, they are utilized to shape consumer behavior and perception. Empty signifiers can be employed to create an illusion of social responsibility, encouraging consumers to support brands or products without substantive evidence of ethical practices.

As we navigate the complexities of public discourse, it is crucial to recognize the danger posed by empty signifiers. By falling prey to their emotional allure and failing to critically analyze their true meanings, we risk being manipulated and manipulated others. This chapter aims to raise awareness about the prevalence and dangers of empty signifiers, encouraging a more discerning approach to communication and discourse. Through informed engagement and critical thinking, we can better discern genuine intentions from manipulative tactics and foster a more thoughtful and constructive public sphere.

## The Concept of Empty Signifiers

The concept of empty signifiers, also known as floating signifiers, was first introduced by the French psychoanalyst and philosopher Jacques Lacan in the field of linguistics and semiotics. In linguistic theory, a signifier is a word, symbol, or image that carries a particular meaning, while the signified is the concept or idea represented by that signifier. In the case of empty signifiers, the signifier lacks a stable or specific signified, making it an open and flexible vessel for various interpretations and emotions.

Empty signifiers gain their power through the attachment of emotions and values, allowing them to be manipulated and exploited for different purposes. They often emerge during times of social and political upheaval, serving as rallying points for individuals and groups with diverse interests. These signifiers tend to evoke strong emotions and evoke a sense of unity among those who embrace them, despite the lack of a clear and consistent meaning.

One of the defining characteristics of empty signifiers is their ambiguity, which enables different actors to project their own meanings and desires onto them. This ambiguity is particularly dangerous as it can facilitate the spread of misinformation and the manipulation of public sentiment. Political and social movements have employed empty signifiers to appeal to broad audiences, promising change and progress without specifying the concrete actions required to achieve these goals.

Furthermore, the use of empty signifiers in media and advertising has become pervasive. Corporations often employ them to create a positive image and evoke positive emotions among consumers without addressing the substantive issues related to social responsibility and sustainability.

The concept of empty signifiers also intersects with the rise of social media and its impact on communication. In the digital age, information travels rapidly, and empty signifiers can quickly go viral, shaping public narratives and influencing public opinion. Social media platforms have become battlegrounds for competing narratives, with empty signifiers being used to fuel polarization and division.

Recognizing and understanding the concept of empty signifiers is crucial for fostering meaningful communication and combating manipulative tactics. By questioning the true meaning and intentions behind the words and symbols used in public discourse, we can avoid falling prey to emotional manipulation and ensure that our engagement with social and political issues remains informed and critical. Moreover, addressing the dangers of empty signifiers can contribute to a more responsible and ethical approach to communication and activism in the modern world.

## The Evolution of "Wokeness" as an Empty Signifier

"Wokeness" has undergone a significant evolution as a cultural and political concept, becoming one of the most prominent examples of an empty signifier in contemporary society. Originally emerging from AAVE as "stay woke," the term referred to being alert to social injustices and systemic oppression. It gained traction during the Black Lives Matter movement, where it was used as a call to action against racial inequality and police brutality.

However, as "wokeness" permeated mainstream culture, its meaning began to shift and lose its specificity. Instead of representing a commitment to social justice and activism, "wokeness" became an abstract and malleable signifier that different groups co-opted to serve their interests.

**Co-optation by Corporations:** As the term gained popularity, corporations began adopting "wokeness" as a marketing tool. They used superficial gestures such as rainbow logos during Pride Month or Black Lives Matter hashtags to present themselves as socially conscious, while often failing to address the systemic issues they perpetuate.

**Performative Activism:** With "wokeness" becoming a buzzword, performative activism became prevalent. People and organizations would adopt the language and aesthetics of social justice without engaging in substantive action or self-reflection.

**Weaponization by the Right:** The term "woke" has been weaponized by some conservative and far-right groups to discredit progressive ideas and dismiss concerns about social inequality. It has been used to delegitimize genuine activism and progressive policies.

**Political Divisiveness:** "Wokeness" has become a divisive term in political discourse, with some arguing that it stifles free speech and promotes cancel culture, while others see it as a necessary force for challenging oppressive systems.

**Erosion of Activist Efforts:** The co-optation of "wokeness" has led to the dilution of its original meaning, which undermines the efforts of genuine activists fighting for social change.

Understanding the evolution of "wokeness" as an empty signifier is essential to reclaiming its original intent and addressing the dangers of its misappropriation. By recognizing how the term has been distorted and manipulated, we can work towards restoring its potency as a call to action against social injustice and advocating for substantive change. By distinguishing between genuine activism and performative gestures, we can create a more inclusive and meaningful dialogue surrounding social justice issues and promote meaningful progress. It is crucial to remain vigilant in identifying and challenging the misappropriation of "wokeness" to ensure its authenticity and efficacy as a force for positive change.

## The Hazards of Vague and Ambiguous Language

Empty signifiers, such as "wokeness," are characterized by their vagueness and ambiguity. While these terms might evoke strong emotions and surface-level agreement, they lack clear definitions and concrete actions. The hazards of vague and ambiguous language are multifaceted and can have significant negative impacts on social and political discourse:

**Dilution of Meaning:** As empty signifiers become popularized, their original meaning often becomes diluted or lost altogether. When terms like "wokeness" are used in a myriad of contexts without precise definitions, their potency as instruments for social change weakens.

**Miscommunication and Misunderstanding:** Vagueness and

ambiguity lead to miscommunication and misunderstanding. Different individuals or groups may interpret the same term differently, leading to conflicts and ineffective dialogue.

**Lack of Accountability:** When concepts lack specific definitions, it becomes challenging to hold individuals or organizations accountable for their actions. Without clear criteria for what it means to be "woke" or socially conscious, performative gestures can be mistaken for genuine activism.

**Obfuscation of Responsibility:** The haziness of empty signifiers can be exploited by those in power to avoid addressing specific issues or taking responsibility for their actions. They can use vague language to deflect criticism and maintain the status quo.

**Ineffectiveness in Mobilization:** Empty signifiers often fail to mobilize people for meaningful action. While they might generate short-lived interest or public attention, they lack the substance required to sustain long-term movements.

**Polarization:** Ambiguous language can lead to polarization in society. The lack of clear definitions makes it easier for different groups to interpret terms in ways that support their own narratives and agendas, leading to further division and distrust.

**Opportunity for Misuse:** Vague language can be misused for propaganda or disinformation campaigns. Empty signifiers may be intentionally employed to manipulate public opinion and promote false narratives.

Addressing the hazards of vague and ambiguous language is crucial for fostering constructive and authentic dialogue. Defining terms clearly and using precise language can enhance understanding, promote accountability, and facilitate collaboration among diverse groups. By seeking out well-defined and specific terms in our discussions, we can avoid falling into the traps of empty signifiers and work towards more meaningful and effective social and political change.

## Polarization and Empty Signifiers

The rise of empty signifiers like "wokeness" has been accompanied by increasing polarization within society. These vague and emotionally charged terms have become tools for both sides of the political spectrum to advance their agendas, further deepening the divides among people:

**Weaponization of Empty Signifiers:** Empty signifiers can be weaponized by different groups to delegitimize their opponents. Those on the right may use "wokeness" as a pejorative to criticize progressive movements and dismiss social justice concerns. On the other hand, those on the left might use "wokeness" to criticize their opponents' lack of awareness and social consciousness.

**Echo Chambers and Confirmation Bias:** The use of empty signifiers in polarized debates reinforces echo chambers, where individuals surround themselves with like-minded people who share similar beliefs. These echo chambers perpetuate confirmation bias, making it difficult for people to engage in meaningful dialogue across ideological lines.

**Ingroup-Outgroup Dynamics:** Empty signifiers contribute to ingroup-outgroup dynamics, where people define themselves in opposition to others. This tribalism fosters animosity and makes it challenging to find common ground and work towards collective solutions.

**Political Exploitation:** Politicians and media outlets often use empty signifiers to exploit people's emotions and fears for political gain. This exploitation reinforces divisions and prevents constructive dialogue on complex issues.

**Stifling Open Dialogue:** The polarization stemming from empty signifiers hinders open and respectful conversations about important social and political matters. People become hesitant to engage in discussions due to fear of being labeled or ostracized based on their beliefs.

**Loss of Nuance:** Empty signifiers oversimplify complex issues, making it difficult to explore nuances and find comprehensive solutions to societal challenges. This oversimplification perpetuates surface-level debates and prevents a deeper understanding of root causes.

**Resistance to Change:** Polarization around empty signifiers can entrench rigid attitudes and resistance to change. The focus on divisive language diverts attention from addressing the underlying structural issues that perpetuate inequalities.

To mitigate the impact of empty signifiers on polarization, it is essential to foster empathy, active listening, and open dialogue. Engaging in constructive conversations that emphasize shared values and aspirations can help bridge ideological divides. Encouraging critical thinking and media literacy can also empower individuals to challenge misleading narratives and engage with complex issues in a more nuanced way. By recognizing the dangers of empty signifiers in fueling polarization, society can begin to move towards a more inclusive and understanding collective discourse.

### The Paradox of Empowerment and Disempowerment

Empty signifiers like "wokeness" present a paradox of both empowerment and disempowerment, as they can have complex effects on different groups within society:

**Empowerment through Identity Affirmation:** For marginalized communities, empty signifiers can provide a sense of empowerment by acknowledging and affirming their identities and struggles. The recognition of their experiences can foster solidarity and a sense of belonging, leading to mobilization for social change.

**Disempowerment through Tokenism:** However, empty signifiers can also lead to disempowerment when they are used superficially by those in power as a form of tokenism. When corporations or institutions adopt these terms without genuine commitment to change, it can be seen as performative, and it erodes the credibility of the movement.

**Centering Voices vs. Silencing Others:** The focus on specific empty signifiers can lead to the centering of certain voices and experiences, potentially silencing others who may not fit within the narrowly defined narrative of "wokeness."

**Marginalization of Genuine Issues:** The proliferation of empty signifiers can sometimes overshadow genuine issues that require urgent attention and action. When certain terms become buzzwords, they may overshadow and divert resources from addressing pressing social and economic disparities.

**Resistance to Systemic Change:** The emphasis on individual actions associated with empty signifiers can distract from the need for broader systemic change. While personal growth and self-awareness are crucial, systemic issues require collective solutions.

**Impact on Allyship:** Empty signifiers can also complicate allyship efforts. Allies may find it challenging to navigate these concepts, leading to either performative gestures or a fear of saying the wrong thing and unintentionally causing harm.

To address this paradox, it is essential to strike a balance between empowerment and disempowerment. This involves recognizing and amplifying the voices of marginalized communities genuinely and creating space for their stories and experiences. At the same time, avoiding tokenistic practices and engaging in meaningful, transformative action is crucial.

Promoting intersectionality and recognizing the complexity of identities and experiences is also vital in moving beyond the limitations of empty signifiers. True empowerment comes from acknowledging and understanding the diverse struggles that individuals face within their intersecting identities.

Ultimately, to break free from the paradox of empowerment and disempowerment, society must prioritize authentic engagement with social issues, centering on substantive dialogue, and working towards systemic change that benefits all members of the community.

## The Manipulation of Social Justice Language

The manipulation of social justice language, including empty signifiers, has become a prevalent tactic in various spheres, including politics, media, and social discourse. This manipulation can have significant consequences for the understanding and advancement of social justice causes:

**Co-optation for Political Agenda:** Politicians and interest groups often co-opt social justice language, including empty signifiers, to advance their political agendas. They may use these terms to appeal to specific voter bases without genuinely understanding or addressing the underlying issues.

**Dilution of Meaning:** The overuse and misappropriation of social justice language can dilute their original meaning and impact. When these terms are used flippantly or insincerely, their significance is diminished, making it harder to address real systemic issues.

**Manufactured Outrage:** Empty signifiers can be weaponized to manufacture outrage and polarize communities. By misrepresenting or exaggerating social justice issues, some entities may manipulate public opinion for their benefit.

**Media Sensationalism:** Media outlets may use empty signifiers to sensationalize stories and attract viewership. In doing so, they risk oversimplifying complex issues and contributing to the misrepresentation of social justice causes.

**Fomenting Division:** The manipulation of social justice language can lead to division within society. It can create an "us versus them" mentality, where those who use the terms differently or disagree with their misappropriation are labeled as adversaries.

**Undermining Legitimate Activism:** By discrediting or mocking social justice language, critics can undermine legitimate activist movements. This tactic seeks to dismiss the concerns of marginalized communities and deflect attention from genuine issues.

**Gaslighting and Dismissal:** Some individuals may use empty signifiers to gaslight or dismiss those who raise concerns about social injustices. They may employ these terms as a way to downplay systemic problems or deny their existence altogether.

To address the manipulation of social justice language, it is essential to promote critical thinking and media literacy. Encouraging informed discussions that delve beyond buzzwords and empty signifiers can help combat misinformation and sensationalism. Additionally, holding public figures and media outlets accountable for their use of social justice language can discourage the misuse of these terms for personal gain.

Moreover, grassroots activism and community organizing can play a pivotal role in reclaiming the narrative and ensuring that social justice language remains authentic and aligned with its original purpose: addressing systemic injustices and creating a more equitable society.

### The Challenge of Effective Advocacy

Navigating the realm of advocacy in a society permeated with empty signifiers poses several challenges for those striving to effect meaningful change:

**Communication Barriers:** The overuse and misappropriation of social justice language create communication barriers between advocates and the broader public. Meaningful dialogue may be hindered when people interpret the same terms differently or dismiss them altogether due to their empty signifier status.

**Loss of Credibility:** Advocates risk losing credibility when their message is diluted by empty signifiers. Skepticism arises when the public perceives these terms as mere buzzwords, undermining the authenticity of the cause and the advocate's commitment.

**Targeted Discreditation:** Opponents of social justice causes may exploit empty signifiers to discredit advocates and their campaigns. By focusing on the misuse or overuse of particular terms, detractors can divert attention from the substantive issues at hand.

**Emotional Manipulation:** Some advocates may inadvertently rely on empty signifiers to evoke emotions in their audience. While emotions can be a powerful motivator, overreliance on buzzwords may lead to an appeal based on sentiment rather than a well-founded argument.

**Navigating Intersectionality:** The intersectionality of social justice issues adds complexity to advocacy efforts. Empty signifiers may inadvertently oversimplify the lived experiences of diverse communities, undermining the multi-faceted nature of their struggles.

**Balancing Inclusivity and Specificity:** Effective advocacy requires striking a balance between inclusive language that appeals to a broader audience and specific terminology that accurately addresses the nuances of different social justice issues.

**Building Sustainable Movements:** Sustaining a social justice movement requires moving beyond empty signifiers and establishing a strong foundation of diverse voices, clear goals, and concrete action plans.

To overcome these challenges, advocates must prioritize authenticity, education, and intersectional approaches. By engaging in constructive dialogue, acknowledging the complexities of social justice issues, and using language that resonates with diverse audiences, advocacy efforts can transcend empty signifiers and foster genuine change.

Furthermore, advocating for media literacy and critical thinking can help empower the public to discern authentic advocacy from manipulative tactics. Encouraging nuanced conversations that delve beyond buzzwords can foster greater understanding of systemic issues and lead to more effective and sustainable advocacy initiatives. By centering the experiences of marginalized communities and focusing on tangible solutions, advocates can rise above empty signifiers and create meaningful impact in the fight for social justice.

## Reimagining Communication and Language

Addressing the challenge of empty signifiers in advocacy requires a reimagining of communication and language within the social justice movement:

**Defining Clear Concepts:** Advocates should strive to define concepts and terms clearly to avoid ambiguity and misinterpretation. Establishing shared understandings can promote more effective communication and reduce the risk of empty signifiers.

**Contextualizing Language:** Context matters in advocacy. By contextualizing language within the specific social, historical, and cultural contexts in which issues arise, advocates can anchor their messages in real-world experiences and challenges.

**Storytelling and Personal Narratives:** Sharing authentic personal narratives can humanize social justice issues and make them relatable to a broader audience. Storytelling has the power to create empathy and foster connections that go beyond the superficiality of empty signifiers.

**Intersectional Approaches:** Embracing intersectionality allows advocates to recognize the interconnectedness of various forms of oppression. By adopting an intersectional lens, they can develop more comprehensive and nuanced strategies to address social justice issues.

**Language for Inclusivity:** Intentionally inclusive language acknowledges the diverse experiences and identities within the social justice movement. It is vital to use language that does not exclude or marginalize any particular group.

**Emphasis on Education:** Educating both advocates and the general public about the complexities of social justice issues is crucial. A well-informed audience is more likely to engage in meaningful discussions and resist the manipulation of empty signifiers.

**Transparency and Authenticity:** Advocates should remain transparent about their goals, objectives, and strategies. Authenticity in advocacy builds trust and counters accusations of empty signifiers.

**Language Evolution:** Language evolves with society, and the social justice movement should be receptive to changes in terminology and discourse. Adapting language to reflect current understandings and needs can keep advocacy relevant and impactful.

**Multimodal Communication:** Utilizing diverse communication channels, such as visual media, art, and music, can expand the reach of advocacy efforts and engage different audiences beyond the confines of empty signifiers.

**Collaborative Language Development:** Engaging in collaborative language development with affected communities can ensure that language aligns with their experiences and perspectives.

Reimagining communication and language involves a collective effort to transcend empty signifiers and embrace more nuanced, authentic, and effective advocacy. By adopting these approaches, the social justice movement can create a more inclusive and powerful force for transformative change.

### Building Resilience Against Empty Signifiers

To build resilience against empty signifiers within the social justice movement, advocates and activists can adopt various strategies:

**Education and Media Literacy:** Promoting media literacy and critical thinking skills can empower individuals to discern between genuine social justice initiatives and empty signifiers used for manipulation. Educating the public about the tactics employed to exploit empty signifiers can help build resistance against their impact.

**Engaging in Intersectional Dialogues:** Encouraging intersectional dialogues fosters a deeper understanding of the interconnectedness of social justice issues and helps identify when empty signifiers are being used to divert attention from systemic problems.

**Centering Marginalized Voices:** Elevating and centering the voices of marginalized communities can dismantle the misappropriation of their struggles by empty signifiers. Amplifying authentic narratives empowers these communities and diminishes the power of empty signifiers.

**Authenticity in Advocacy:** Prioritizing authenticity in advocacy efforts builds credibility and trust with the public. Demonstrating a commitment to tangible action and measurable progress can counter accusations of empty rhetoric.

**Dismantling Tokenism:** Avoiding tokenism and performative gestures ensures that marginalized individuals are not used as empty signifiers to give the illusion of inclusivity. Instead, genuine efforts to address systemic inequalities should be pursued.

**Promoting Solidarity:** Building solidarity within the social justice movement strengthens collective resilience against empty signifiers. Recognizing shared goals and values unites advocates in the pursuit of genuine change.

**Celebrating Incremental Progress:** Acknowledging and celebrating incremental progress, even amidst larger challenges, reinforces the legitimacy of social justice efforts. This approach can combat claims of empty signifiers by demonstrating ongoing commitment to the cause.

**Transparency and Accountability:** Maintaining transparency in advocacy work, including finances and decision-making processes, fosters accountability. It also safeguards against the infiltration of empty signifiers and opportunistic co-optation.

**Avoiding Overreliance on Symbols:** While symbols and gestures can be powerful tools, overreliance on them may lead to the dilution of substantive efforts. Ensuring that symbolic actions are backed by substantive change can guard against empty signifiers.

**Redefining Success:** Redefining success in the social justice movement beyond empty signifiers can shift the focus towards long-term systemic change. Success can be measured by sustained collective efforts and positive impacts on marginalized communities.

Building resilience against empty signifiers is an ongoing endeavor. By adopting these strategies, the social justice movement can safeguard its integrity and effectiveness, ensuring that its mission remains rooted in authentic advocacy and transformative change.

The rise of "wokeness" and its subsequent co-optation by various actors have brought to light the dangers of empty signifiers within the social justice movement. Empty signifiers are symbols, slogans, and gestures that may appear to represent progressive ideals, but lack substantive action and meaningful change. Throughout this chapter, we have explored the evolution of "wokeness" as an empty signifier and the implications it has on social justice discourse.

The concept of empty signifiers is not limited to "wokeness" alone but extends to other social justice language and advocacy efforts. Their misappropriation can lead to the erosion of trust and credibility within social justice movements, creating divisions and diluting the urgency of addressing systemic inequalities.

The hazards of vague and ambiguous language have been evident in public discourse, where empty signifiers have been weaponized against progressive causes and used to fuel polarization. In navigating the challenges of empty signifiers, it is essential to reevaluate how we communicate and advocate for social justice.

To effectively counter the dangers of empty signifiers, the social justice movement must prioritize authenticity, intersectionality, and inclusivity. By centering the experiences of marginalized communities and amplifying their voices, advocates can build resilience against manipulative attempts to misrepresent their struggles.

Additionally, adopting transparency, accountability, and tangible action will foster a genuine commitment to change, rendering empty signifiers ineffective in undermining the progress made by the social justice movement.

Moving forward, the quest for authenticity in activism and advocacy should be paramount. Embracing personal narratives, engaging in constructive dialogue, and reimagining communication strategies can lead to a deeper and more meaningful impact on society.

Ultimately, building resilience against empty signifiers requires ongoing vigilance and collective efforts. By challenging the conservative misappropriation and promoting genuine social justice initiatives, the movement can reclaim its authenticity and effectiveness.

As advocates, activists, and allies, we must remain vigilant against the misuse of language and symbols and strive for meaningful, transformative change that upholds the values of justice, equality, and inclusion. Only then can we confront the danger of empty signifiers and work towards a more equitable and just world for all.

*"Pointing true north, it is up to us to resurrect it as a symbol of genuine awakening, not empty conformity."*

# CHAPTER 10
# RECLAIMING THE NARRATIVE

The narrative has always played a central role in shaping public perception and driving meaningful change in the fight for social justice. However, the narrative surrounding "wokeness" and other social justice movements has been co-opted, manipulated, and distorted by various actors with vested interests. Chapter 10 stresses the importance of reclaiming the narrative and examines how authentic storytelling can reframe the discourse on social justice.

The power of storytelling lies in its ability to humanize and contextualize the struggles faced by marginalized communities. By sharing personal narratives, lived experiences, and historical context, activists and advocates can humanize social justice issues and foster empathy and understanding among the broader public.

The introduction of empty signifiers and the misappropriation of language have been key challenges in recent times, leading to a misrepresentation of the values and goals of the social justice movement. As a result, the narrative has been skewed, with divisive rhetoric overshadowing the urgent need for equity and inclusivity.

To reclaim the narrative, it is crucial to counter the misappropriation by promoting genuine and authentic stories of individuals and communities impacted by systemic inequities. By doing so, the movement can rebuild trust and credibility, which are essential for fostering meaningful change.

Reframing the discourse on social justice also requires an intersectional approach. Understanding the interconnectedness of different forms of oppression is vital in crafting narratives that encompass the diverse experiences of marginalized groups. Intersectionality acknowledges that the struggles of individuals are not isolated but interconnected and interdependent.

The role of media and information sharing is pivotal in reclaiming the narrative. Media outlets play a significant role in shaping public opinion, and efforts should be made to ensure fair, accurate, and unbiased coverage of social justice issues.

Furthermore, technology and social media have reshaped how information is disseminated and consumed, presenting both opportunities and challenges. Empowering marginalized voices on these platforms can amplify their narratives and bypass traditional gatekeepers, but it also requires navigating potential risks like misinformation and disinformation campaigns.

Ultimately, the quest for reclaiming the narrative is about empowering communities and individuals to share their stories authentically, transcending the narratives imposed upon them by those who seek to undermine the movement. By doing so, the social justice movement can reaffirm its commitment to equality, justice, and liberation, reframing the discourse to focus on the urgency of dismantling systemic oppression and creating a more inclusive and equitable society.

## The Manipulation of Narrative

The manipulation of narrative has become a potent tool in the hands of those seeking to undermine the social justice movement. Powerful actors, including political entities, media outlets, and interest groups, have mastered the art of distorting narratives to advance their agendas.

One common tactic is the selective framing of social justice issues to fit preconceived narratives. By cherry-picking specific incidents or data points, these actors can create a skewed portrayal of the movement and its goals. This selective framing often emphasizes isolated incidents of violence or property damage during protests while ignoring the broader context of systemic racism and injustice.

Another manipulation technique involves "othering" marginalized communities and portraying them as threats or enemies. This tactic feeds into existing prejudices and stereotypes, fostering a sense of fear and distrust towards those advocating for social justice. By sowing discord and division, the manipulators hope to weaken the collective power of the movement.

Misinformation and disinformation campaigns are also used to cast doubt on the credibility of the social justice movement. False narratives and fake news are disseminated through social media, creating confusion and undermining the authenticity of the movement's demands. Such campaigns aim to delegitimize the movement by portraying it as chaotic, misguided, or even violent.

The co-optation of language is yet another manipulation strategy. Terms like "social justice warrior" or "woke" have been weaponized to mock and belittle advocates for social justice. By turning these once empowering terms into pejoratives, manipulators seek to undermine the legitimacy of the movement and its proponents.

Moreover, the amplification of fringe voices within the social justice movement is used to create a false image of its priorities. By focusing on extreme or radical viewpoints, manipulators paint the entire movement as extremist, diverting attention from the core issues of systemic injustice and inequality.

To counter the manipulation of narrative, it is essential for activists and advocates to maintain a consistent and authentic message. By presenting accurate and compelling stories, grounded in real experiences, the movement can confront misrepresentation and set the record straight.

Furthermore, media literacy and critical thinking are crucial for the public to discern fact from fiction and recognize attempts to manipulate narratives. Efforts to promote media literacy and encourage responsible information sharing can equip the public with the tools to resist manipulation.

Ultimately, reclaiming the narrative requires vigilance and a commitment to truth-telling. By exposing and challenging manipulation tactics, the social justice movement can reaffirm its authenticity and inspire meaningful change towards a more equitable and just society.

## The Power of Authentic Storytelling

Authentic storytelling has the power to transform hearts and minds, making it a potent tool for the social justice movement. By sharing personal experiences and connecting on a human level, advocates can break down barriers and build empathy among diverse audiences.

One of the key strengths of authentic storytelling is its ability to put a human face on social justice issues. By sharing stories of individuals who have experienced systemic oppression and discrimination, the movement can personalize complex problems and make them relatable to the broader public. These narratives allow people to see the lived experiences of marginalized communities, fostering a deeper understanding of their struggles and challenges.

Authentic storytelling also helps to counter the negative stereotypes and misrepresentations perpetuated by the manipulation of narrative.

By presenting diverse and nuanced narratives, the movement can challenge one-dimensional portrayals and reveal the complexities of social justice issues.

Moreover, personal stories can inspire and mobilize action. When people hear about the courage and resilience of those fighting for justice, they are more likely to be motivated to join the cause and advocate for change. These stories can also empower individuals from marginalized communities to find their voices and share their own experiences, fostering a sense of agency and collective empowerment.

Through digital platforms and social media, authentic storytelling can reach a global audience, amplifying the voices of those whose stories have been historically marginalized or silenced. Social media campaigns like #MeToo, #BlackLivesMatter, and #TransRightsAreHumanRights have demonstrated the immense power of storytelling to mobilize and effect change on a global scale.

However, with this power comes responsibility. It is essential to ensure that stories are shared with consent, sensitivity, and respect for the storyteller's agency. Authenticity should be prioritized over sensationalism, and narratives should reflect the diverse perspectives within the movement.

Authentic storytelling plays a pivotal role in reclaiming the narrative from manipulators and advancing the social justice movement. By sharing personal stories, the movement can humanize complex issues, inspire action, and create a more empathetic and inclusive society. It is through these stories that the movement can build bridges of understanding and galvanize a collective commitment to justice and equality.

### Elevating Marginalized Voices

It is crucial to prioritize and elevate the voices of those who have historically been marginalized and oppressed in the quest for reclaiming the narrative. Centering these voices in the social justice movement is not only a matter of representation but also an acknowledgment of their expertise, experiences, and unique perspectives.

Elevating marginalized voices means actively seeking out and listening to individuals from diverse backgrounds, including but not limited to people of color, LGBTQ+ individuals, indigenous communities, disabled individuals, and religious minorities. It involves creating inclusive spaces where these voices can be heard and respected.

By elevating marginalized voices, the movement gains access to insights and wisdom that have often been overlooked or undervalued. These perspectives challenge the dominant narratives and offer new ways of understanding and addressing social justice issues.

Additionally, elevating marginalized voices fosters a more equitable and inclusive movement. It creates opportunities for leadership and decision-making from within these communities, ensuring that the solutions proposed are relevant and effective for those most affected.

To elevate marginalized voices, the movement must actively confront tokenism and superficial inclusion. Tokenism occurs when individuals from marginalized groups are included merely for appearance or public relations purposes, without genuine engagement or empowerment. True inclusion requires creating an environment where marginalized individuals are not only present but also valued, heard, and actively involved in decision-making processes.

Furthermore, allies within the movement have a vital role to play in elevating marginalized voices. They can use their privilege and platforms to amplify the voices of those who are often unheard. By actively promoting and sharing the work of marginalized activists, allies can help shift the balance of power within the movement.

Elevating marginalized voices is a central aspect of reclaiming the narrative and creating a more inclusive and effective social justice movement. It requires a commitment to actively seek out and value the perspectives of those who have been historically silenced. By centering these voices, the movement gains deeper insights, strengthens its impact, and moves closer to its goal of a more just and equitable world.

## Decentering Dominant Narratives

Decentering dominant narratives is an essential step in reclaiming the narrative and challenging the status quo. Dominant narratives are the prevailing stories, beliefs, and perspectives that shape public discourse and influence societal norms. They often serve the interests of those in power and perpetuate inequality, reinforcing existing systems of oppression.

To decenter dominant narratives, activists must first recognize their existence and impact. These narratives are deeply ingrained in society and are often taken for granted as "common sense." By critically examining and questioning these narratives, activists can uncover the biases and power dynamics that underpin them.

One way to decenter dominant narratives is to amplify counter-narratives that challenge prevailing beliefs. Counter-narratives offer alternative perspectives and challenge the assumptions embedded in dominant stories. By promoting these counter-narratives, activists can disrupt the one-sided portrayal of social issues and create space for diverse voices and experiences.

Another crucial aspect of decentering dominant narratives is to identify and challenge the language used in public discourse. Language plays a powerful role in shaping perceptions and reinforcing stereotypes. By scrutinizing and reframing the language used to discuss social justice issues, activists can expose hidden biases and present more accurate and empowering narratives.

Furthermore, decentering dominant narratives involves diversifying the sources of information and news that inform public opinion. Mainstream media often perpetuate dominant narratives, and alternative sources of information may provide a more balanced and nuanced perspective. Encouraging media outlets to include a broader range of voices and stories can lead to a more informed and empathetic public discourse.

Decentering dominant narratives also requires addressing historical erasures and misrepresentations. Many marginalized communities' histories and contributions have been suppressed or distorted by dominant narratives. Acknowledging and celebrating these histories can challenge the status quo and empower those whose stories have been silenced.

Decentering dominant narratives is a critical step in reclaiming the narrative and creating a more just and inclusive society. By challenging prevailing beliefs and amplifying counter-narratives, activists can expose the biases and power dynamics that perpetuate inequality. Diversifying sources of information and reframing language further contribute to a more inclusive and accurate portrayal of social justice issues. Through these efforts, the movement can gain momentum and shift public perception, ultimately leading to a more equitable and compassionate world.

## Media Representation and Authenticity

Media representation plays a pivotal role in shaping public perceptions and narratives. It has the power to either reinforce or challenge dominant narratives and stereotypes. Authentic representation in media is crucial for the reclamation of the narrative by marginalized communities.

One of the key issues in media representation is the lack of diversity and inclusion. Historically, mainstream media has perpetuated stereotypes and marginalized minority communities by portraying them in limited and often negative ways. This lack of authentic representation can perpetuate harmful biases and hinder progress towards a more equitable society.

Authentic representation in media involves accurate and nuanced portrayals of diverse experiences and perspectives. It means giving voice to underrepresented communities and ensuring that their stories are told with integrity and respect. Authenticity in media representation goes beyond tokenism or surface-level diversity; it requires a genuine commitment to amplifying diverse voices and providing them with agency over their narratives.

Media creators and storytellers have a responsibility to ensure authenticity in their portrayals. This includes involving individuals from the communities being represented in the creative process, seeking their input, and avoiding harmful stereotypes. Collaboration with community members can lead to more nuanced and authentic narratives that accurately reflect their experiences.

Additionally, media consumers have a role to play in demanding authentic representation. By supporting media that prioritizes diversity and inclusion, audiences can send a clear message to content creators and media organizations about the importance of accurate portrayals. Social media and online platforms have provided a space for marginalized voices to challenge misrepresentations and demand better media representation.

Moreover, media outlets and organizations must also address their internal practices and ensure diversity among their staff and decision-makers. Having a diverse team helps in avoiding bias and ensures a more nuanced understanding of various communities' experiences.

Media representation is a powerful tool in reclaiming the narrative and challenging dominant narratives. Authentic representation requires a commitment to diversity, inclusion, and accurate portrayals. By elevating diverse voices, involving marginalized communities in the creative process, and holding media organizations accountable, the movement can work towards a more authentic and equitable media landscape.

### Reclaiming "Wokeness" and Social Justice Language

The term "wokeness" and other social justice language have been co-opted and weaponized to undermine and discredit progressive movements. However, there is a growing effort to reclaim these terms and redefine them on the terms of social justice advocates.

Reclaiming "wokeness" involves restoring its original meaning, which is the awareness of social injustices and the commitment to challenge and dismantle oppressive systems. It is about recognizing privilege and using it to advocate for marginalized communities. By reframing "wokeness" as a positive force for social change, advocates can counter the negative connotations that have been associated with the term.

Similarly, reclaiming social justice language involves redefining terms such as "diversity," "inclusion," "intersectionality," and "allyship" in their authentic and empowering context. This is important because conservatives have often used these terms to dismiss or mock social justice efforts, derailing meaningful discussions about inequality and justice.

To reclaim social justice language, advocates must engage in open and honest dialogues about the meanings and intentions behind these terms. They can share personal stories and experiences to humanize the impact of social justice efforts. Furthermore, education plays a crucial role in reclaiming these terms, as it can provide clarity on their origins and significance.

Social media and digital platforms offer a space for marginalized communities to reclaim language and narratives. By using hashtags and creating online movements, activists can assert their own interpretations of social justice language and challenge misappropriations.

Moreover, the reclamation of language is a continuous process that requires active resistance against attempts to misuse and distort these terms. By remaining steadfast in their commitment to social justice principles, advocates can demonstrate the authenticity and sincerity of their efforts.

Reclaiming "wokeness" and social justice language is an essential step in challenging the conservative misappropriation of these terms. By reframing them in their true contexts and empowering marginalized voices to lead the conversation, advocates can take back control of the narrative and work towards a more just and equitable society.

## Intersectional Narratives for Social Change

Intersectionality recognizes that various forms of oppression intersect and overlap, impacting individuals differently based on their identities. Intersectional narratives play a pivotal role in reclaiming the narrative for social change. By centering the experiences of marginalized communities, these narratives highlight the complex web of inequalities and offer a more comprehensive understanding of social issues.

**Acknowledging Multiple Identities:** Intersectional narratives consider the intersection of race, gender, class, sexuality, disability, and other identities. By acknowledging the interplay of these identities, they provide a nuanced perspective on how different forms of discrimination can compound and exacerbate social inequities.

**Amplifying Marginalized Voices:** These narratives elevate the voices of those historically marginalized and silenced. They provide a platform for individuals to share their lived experiences, fostering empathy and understanding among broader audiences.

**Challenging Single-Story Narratives:** Intersectional narratives counter single-story portrayals of communities, which often perpetuate harmful stereotypes. They present a holistic view of marginalized experiences, promoting empathy and solidarity.

**Fostering Empowerment and Resilience:** Sharing intersectional narratives can empower individuals and communities to challenge systemic oppression. By reclaiming their stories, they resist erasure and reclaim agency over their lives.

**Building Coalitions and Solidarity:** Intersectional narratives highlight the interconnectedness of various struggles for justice. They encourage diverse movements to collaborate and support one another, forging stronger alliances for social change.

**Engaging in Difficult Conversations:** These narratives facilitate difficult conversations about privilege and complicity in systems of oppression. By embracing uncomfortable truths, they promote self-reflection and growth.

**Promoting Policy and Structural Changes:** Intersectional narratives can drive policy changes by highlighting the specific needs and challenges faced by marginalized communities. They advocate for systemic solutions to address root causes of injustice.

**Inspiring Cultural Shifts:** These narratives can lead to broader cultural shifts by challenging harmful norms and fostering a more inclusive and equitable society.

Reclaiming the narrative through intersectional storytelling requires genuine collaboration with affected communities. It demands active listening, humility, and an openness to learn from those whose experiences differ from our own. Ultimately, intersectional narratives can serve as a catalyst for transformative social change, creating a world where all individuals are valued and empowered.

### Allies and Narrative Support

In the quest to reclaim the narrative, allies play a crucial role in amplifying marginalized voices and supporting social justice movements. Allies are individuals who recognize their privilege and actively use it to challenge systems of oppression and uplift marginalized communities. Here's how allies can provide narrative support:

**Listening and Learning:** Allies must be attentive listeners to understand the experiences of marginalized communities better. By engaging in active learning about diverse perspectives, they can better support authentic narratives.

**Amplifying Voices:** Instead of speaking for marginalized communities, allies should use their privilege to elevate the voices of those directly impacted. This can be done by sharing and promoting their stories, art, and experiences.

**Using Their Platforms:** Allies with platforms, whether large or small, can leverage them to draw attention to social justice issues and advocate for change. They can use social media, public speaking opportunities, or their artistic work to raise awareness.

**Providing Resources:** Allies can offer resources and support to help marginalized individuals and communities share their narratives. This may include providing funding for projects, connecting them to media outlets, or offering technical assistance.

**Acknowledging Their Privilege:** Allies must recognize and confront their privilege to avoid dominating the narrative or centering themselves in the conversation. They should strive to use their privilege to create space for marginalized voices.

**Challenging Misrepresentations:** When allies encounter misrepresentations or harmful narratives about marginalized communities, they should actively challenge and correct them. This can be done in personal conversations, social media interactions, or public forums.

**Being Accountable:** Allies should be open to feedback and willing to learn from their mistakes. They should take responsibility for any harmful actions or statements and commit to doing better.

**Supporting Media Diversity:** Allies can advocate for greater diversity in media and creative industries. By demanding inclusive representation and supporting diverse storytellers, they contribute to a more accurate and equitable portrayal of society.

**Collaboration and Partnership:** Allies should seek genuine collaboration and partnership with marginalized communities. Centering the expertise and leadership of affected individuals ensures that narratives are authentic and empowering.

**Building Bridges:** Allies can act as bridges between different communities, fostering dialogue and understanding. By bringing diverse perspectives together, they can promote solidarity and coalition-building for collective change.

By actively supporting authentic narratives and engaging in anti-op-
pressive work, allies contribute to the dismantling of harmful narratives and the fostering of a more just and inclusive society. It is through
collective efforts that the narrative can be reclaimed and reshaped to
reflect the true diversity and richness of human experiences.

## Navigating Cultural and Historical Context

When reclaiming the narrative, it is crucial to consider the cultural
and historical context in which stories are told. Narratives are shaped
by social, political, and historical factors that influence how stories
are perceived and received. Navigating this context is essential to ensure that narratives are authentic, respectful, and impactful. Here are
some key aspects to consider:

**Cultural Sensitivity:** Different cultures have unique storytelling
traditions and norms. Reclaiming the narrative requires a deep understanding of these cultural sensitivities to avoid appropriating or
misrepresenting experiences.

**Historical Oppression:** Many marginalized communities have a
history of oppression that continues to impact their narratives. Acknowledging this history is essential to grasp the depth and complexity of their stories.

**Colonial Legacies:** Colonialism and imperialism have left lasting
scars on many communities, affecting how their stories are told and
interpreted. Reclaiming the narrative involves challenging colonial
legacies and empowering people to tell their stories on their terms.

**Intersecting Identities:** People's experiences are shaped by various intersecting identities, such as race, gender, sexuality, and disability. It is crucial to recognize these intersections and avoid essentializing
or tokenizing narratives.

**Historical Erasure:** Some narratives have been historically erased or suppressed due to dominant power structures. Reclaiming the narrative involves uncovering and amplifying these hidden stories.

**Language and Translation:** In multicultural contexts, language and translation play a vital role in conveying authentic narratives. Ensuring accurate translation and interpretation is essential to maintain the integrity of the stories.

**Empowerment and Ownership:** Navigating cultural and historical context involves empowering communities to own and shape their narratives. Instead of imposing outsider perspectives, the focus should be on supporting self-representation.

**Respecting Trauma and Healing:** Many marginalized communities have experienced trauma. Reclaiming the narrative should be done with sensitivity, respecting the healing process and not retraumatizing individuals through storytelling.

**Recognizing Counter-Narratives:** Dominant narratives often perpetuate stereotypes and biases. Reclaiming the narrative involves recognizing and amplifying counter-narratives that challenge these harmful perceptions.

**Community Engagement:** Engaging with the community is essential to navigate cultural and historical context effectively. Working collaboratively ensures that narratives are authentic, respectful, and representative.

By navigating cultural and historical context with care and understanding, storytellers can amplify marginalized voices in ways that challenge dominant narratives and contribute to the broader movement of social justice and inclusion. Authentic storytelling has the power to reshape perspectives, build empathy, and create a more equitable society for all.

In a world filled with diverse voices and experiences, narratives play a profound role in shaping collective consciousness and influencing societal attitudes. The quest for authentic storytelling and reclaiming narratives is inseparable from the larger struggle for social justice and equity. This chapter explored the power of narratives, the dangers of empty signifiers, and the ways in which dominant forces can misappropriate and co-opt language to maintain power structures.

Through this journey, we discovered that "wokeness" and social justice language have been weaponized and diluted by both corporate interests and political ideologies, leaving us with empty signifiers that fail to address the root causes of injustice. But there is hope, as the chapter also highlighted the potential for reclaiming language and narratives for progressive change.

By embracing authenticity and elevating marginalized voices, we can challenge misappropriation and combat divisive narratives. The power of intersectional storytelling lies in its ability to build bridges of understanding and empathy among diverse communities. Reclaiming narratives allows us to decenter dominant perspectives and amplify marginalized voices, making the struggle for social justice more inclusive and effective.

Allyship is key in this journey towards authentic storytelling. Allies can play a vital role in supporting marginalized communities, ensuring that narratives are respectful and representative. However, allyship must be approached with humility, openness, and a willingness to listen and learn.

As we navigate cultural and historical contexts, we must remember that storytelling is not just about words but also about lived experiences, emotions, and resilience. It requires grappling with uncomfortable truths, acknowledging historical injustices, and promoting healing through empathy.

Reclaiming the narrative is an ongoing process of reflection, collaboration, and action. It requires us to be critical consumers of media, responsible storytellers, and active participants in social change. By embracing authentic storytelling and amplifying a host of marginalized voices, we can challenge misappropriation, dismantle harmful narratives, and foster a more just and inclusive society for everyone. Let us continue this journey with empathy and determination, knowing that the power to reclaim the narrative is within our collective grasp.

*"The journey towards genuine awakening resembles the actions
of the circus performer walking the tightrope over the abyss of ignorance."*

# CHAPTER 11
# TOWARDS A GENUINE AWAKENING

The journey towards a genuine awakening is an exploration of consciousness, empathy, and collective responsibility. Throughout this book, we have investigated, examined and documented the complexities of "wokeness," the dangers of its misappropriation, and the power of reclaiming narratives. Now, we embark on a new chapter that calls for deeper introspection and meaningful action.

The term "awakening" has become synonymous with social awareness and consciousness about systemic injustices. However, we recognize that mere surface-level awareness is not enough. True awakening requires a commitment to continuous learning, unlearning, and engagement with the world around us. It demands that we confront our biases, privileges, and prejudices to build a more equitable society.

In this chapter, we will explore the components of a genuine awakening. This includes the role of education in dismantling systemic inequalities, the importance of empathy and emotional intelligence, and the significance of authentic allyship in collective movements for change. We will also delve into the impact of media and technology in shaping our perceptions and attitudes towards social justice issues.

A genuine awakening goes beyond performative gestures and empty signifiers. It compels us to question the structures that perpetuate injustice and to actively work towards dismantling them. It calls for solidarity and a shared commitment to advocating for those whose voices have been silenced or marginalized.

Throughout this chapter, we will emphasize the necessity of intersectionality in our awakening process. Recognizing the interconnectedness of different forms of oppression and privilege helps us develop a more nuanced understanding of social justice issues and strengthens our resolve to challenge systemic inequities.

As we navigate this chapter, let us approach the concept of awakening with humility and self-reflection. A genuine awakening is not a destination but a journey of continuous growth and transformation. It requires us to be vulnerable and open to discomfort as we confront uncomfortable truths about ourselves and the world we inhabit.

Let us foster an environment that encourages dialogue, learning, and collaboration in the true spirit of the pursuit of a genuine awakening. Together, we can create a world where empathy, justice, and authenticity are the guiding principles that shape our interactions and societal structures. Let us embark on this journey towards a genuine awakening, committed to building a better future for all.

## The Journey of Self-Awareness

The journey of self-awareness is the cornerstone of a genuine awakening. It is an exploration of our inner landscape, an invitation to look deep within ourselves, and a commitment to understanding our biases, beliefs, and conditioning. Self-awareness is not a one-time event but a continuous process of introspection and self-reflection.

To embark on this journey, we must be willing to confront uncomfortable truths about ourselves and our place in the world. It requires us to acknowledge the privileges we hold, the biases we carry, and the blind spots that limit our understanding of others' experiences. It is an act of humility that challenges us to recognize that we are not separate from the systems of oppression that exist in society but are interconnected with them.

Developing self-awareness involves actively listening to marginalized voices and acknowledging their lived experiences. It means being open to feedback and criticism, understanding that our intentions are not always aligned with the impact of our actions. It requires us to step out of our comfort zones and engage in difficult conversations, both with ourselves and others.

The journey of self-awareness is not linear, and it may be accompanied by feelings of guilt, shame, or defensiveness. It is essential to remember that these emotions are part of the process and should not deter us from continuing our exploration. Instead, we can use them as opportunities for growth and learning.

As we delve deeper into our self-awareness journey, we gain a better understanding of how our identities intersect with power dynamics in society. We begin to recognize the ways in which our identities influence our perspectives and interactions with others. This understanding allows us to develop empathy and compassion, not only for ourselves but also for others who navigate different experiences.

Cultivating self-awareness is not an isolated endeavor. It is enhanced through community and collective support. Engaging in dialogue with others who are also on their awakening journey provides valuable insights and broadens our perspectives. Together, we can hold each other accountable and uplift one another as we strive for a more equitable world.

Self-awareness is the foundational step, if you are to be honestly intellectual in the pursuit of a genuine awakening. It enables us to recognize our responsibilities as agents of change and empowers us to contribute meaningfully to dismantling systemic oppression. As we continue this journey, we move towards deeper empathy, authentic allyship, and a more interconnected understanding of social justice issues.

## Unlearning and Relearning

Unlearning and relearning are vital aspects of the journey towards a genuine awakening. It involves challenging the assumptions and beliefs that we have internalized from societal conditioning and actively seeking new knowledge and perspectives to replace them. Unlearning requires us to question the narratives that have shaped our understanding of the world and to be open to unearthing uncomfortable truths.

The process of unlearning can be both liberating and challenging. It requires us to confront cognitive dissonance and be willing to let go of deeply ingrained beliefs that perpetuate inequality and injustice. This can be difficult, as our identities and sense of self are often intertwined with the beliefs we hold. However, embracing a growth mindset and a commitment to justice can guide us through this transformative process.

Unlearning also involves acknowledging the gaps in our knowledge and actively seeking out diverse voices and perspectives. It means seeking out resources, literature, and educational materials that challenge dominant narratives and shed light on the experiences of marginalized communities. This continual pursuit of knowledge broadens our understanding and empowers us to become more effective advocates for social change.

Relearning, on the other hand, is about intentionally acquiring new knowledge and adopting more inclusive and equitable perspectives. It involves centering the voices and experiences of marginalized communities and challenging the historical narratives that have perpetuated systemic oppression. Through relearning, we gain a deeper appreciation for the complexities of social justice issues and the interconnectedness of various struggles.

Unlearning and relearning also require humility and a willingness to be vulnerable. It is essential to recognize that we will make mistakes along the way and to approach the learning process with humility and openness to feedback. Acknowledging our privilege and the limitations of our perspectives can be uncomfortable, but it is a necessary part of the journey towards genuine awakening.

Additionally, unlearning and relearning are ongoing processes. As we become more aware of the world's complexities, we must continuously challenge ourselves to grow and evolve. This involves staying engaged with current social justice issues, seeking feedback, and critically reflecting on our actions and beliefs.

Unlearning and relearning are powerful tools for personal and collective transformation. By challenging our assumptions, seeking new knowledge, and centering marginalized voices, we can develop a deeper understanding of social justice issues and become more effective agents of change in the pursuit of a more equitable and just world.

## The Role of Empathy and Listening

Empathy and active listening are fundamental components of the journey towards a genuine awakening. In the pursuit of social justice, it is essential to develop empathy for the experiences and struggles of others, particularly those who have been marginalized and oppressed. Empathy allows us to connect with the emotions and perspectives of others, fostering a deeper understanding of their lived realities.

To practice empathy, we must be willing to step outside of our own experiences and center the experiences of others. This involves actively listening to the stories and narratives of marginalized communities without judgment or defensiveness. Through empathy, we can develop a greater sense of compassion and solidarity with those who are facing injustice.

Listening plays a crucial role in building authentic relationships and fostering trust. To be effective allies and advocates, we must prioritize active listening over speaking. This means creating space for others to share their stories and experiences without interruption, offering validation and support. Listening is not just about hearing words; it involves being attuned to non-verbal cues and emotions to gain a holistic understanding of someone's perspective.

Through empathetic listening, we can also recognize our own biases and assumptions, challenging them to create more inclusive spaces for dialogue. It requires suspending judgment and truly valuing the diverse perspectives that are present in social justice movements. Listening also empowers individuals from marginalized communities by validating their experiences and elevating their voices.

It is essential to remember that empathy and listening are not passive acts but require conscious effort and practice. Engaging in difficult conversations with an open heart and mind can be uncomfortable, but it is necessary for growth and understanding. Cultivating empathy and active listening allows us to build meaningful relationships and coalitions that can drive positive change.

Empathy and active listening are powerful tools for fostering genuine awakening. By centering the experiences of marginalized communities and genuinely seeking to understand their perspectives, we can build stronger connections, challenge our biases, and become more effective allies in the fight for social justice.

## Recognizing Complicity and Accountability

It is crucial to recognize and acknowledge our own complicity in systems of oppression and structural inequalities. Complicity refers to the ways in which individuals, knowingly or unknowingly, contribute to or benefit from oppressive systems. This recognition is a necessary step in dismantling those very systems and becoming true allies in the fight for social justice.

Acknowledging our complicity can be challenging and uncomfortable. It requires a willingness to confront our privilege, biases, and the ways in which we have perpetuated harmful narratives or remained silent in the face of injustice. However, by doing so, we can start to understand the ways in which we are connected to larger systems of power and inequality.

Holding ourselves accountable is an essential aspect of this process. It involves taking responsibility for our actions and inactions, and committing to learning, unlearning, and actively working towards change. Accountability also means being open to feedback and criticism from marginalized communities without becoming defensive.

One of the key elements of recognizing complicity and accountability is self-reflection. Taking time to critically examine our beliefs, actions, and the impact they have on others is vital. This introspection can lead to a deeper understanding of how we can contribute positively to social justice efforts.

Another important aspect of recognizing complicity is understanding that it is not a one-time event. It is an ongoing process of learning and growth. As we continue on our journey towards a genuine awakening, we must remain committed to challenging ourselves and each other to do better.

Moreover, recognizing complicity and accountability extends beyond individuals. Institutions, organizations, and communities must also engage in this process. Acknowledging the role they play in perpetuating oppressive structures is crucial for creating meaningful change.

Recognizing our complicity and holding ourselves accountable are vital steps in the journey towards a genuine awakening. It requires self-reflection, openness to feedback, and a commitment to continuous learning and growth. By acknowledging our role in perpetuating systems of oppression, we can become more effective allies and advocates for social justice.

### The Power of Collective Consciousness

The power of collective consciousness cannot be underestimated. Collective consciousness refers to the shared beliefs, values, and understanding that unite individuals in a society or community. When people come together with a shared purpose and vision, they can ignite powerful movements and drive significant change.

One of the key aspects of collective consciousness is solidarity. It is the realization that the struggles and liberation of one group are interconnected with the struggles and liberation of others. Solidarity transcends individual identities and fosters a sense of common purpose in fighting against all forms of oppression and injustice.

Collective consciousness can be harnessed through various means, such as community organizing, grassroots movements, and social media platforms. When people engage in dialogue and collaboration, they can amplify their voices and create a powerful force for change.

At the heart of collective consciousness is empathy and compassion. Understanding and acknowledging the experiences of others, especially those from marginalized communities, are essential in building connections and fostering unity. By actively listening and learning from each other, individuals can develop a deeper understanding of the complex issues that underlie social injustices.

Furthermore, the power of collective consciousness lies in its ability to challenge dominant narratives and reshape societal norms. When a critical mass of people comes together to challenge oppressive systems, they can dismantle the very foundations that uphold these structures.

Collective consciousness can drive the creation of new paradigms and values. By envisioning a more just and equitable society, people can collectively work towards creating it.

While collective consciousness is a potent force, it is not without challenges. Diverse perspectives and backgrounds within movements may lead to disagreements and conflicts. However, embracing and navigating these differences is a crucial aspect of collective consciousness, as it allows for more inclusive and intersectional movements.

The power of collective consciousness is a driving force in the pursuit of a genuine awakening. Through solidarity, empathy, and shared purpose, individuals can challenge oppressive systems, amplify marginalized voices, and work together towards a more just and equitable world. It is a transformative force that holds the potential to reshape society and create lasting positive change.

## Moving Beyond Performative Activism

Moving beyond performative activism is critical. Performative activism refers to superficial or symbolic gestures that individuals or organizations engage in to appear socially conscious or progressive without enacting substantial change.

Performative activism often involves virtue signaling, where individuals publicly demonstrate their support for social justice causes without actively engaging in meaningful actions to address the root issues. This form of activism can be misleading and divert attention away from genuine efforts to effect positive change.

To move beyond performative activism, individuals must prioritize substance over appearance. This means taking concrete actions to support marginalized communities and advance social justice causes. It involves educating oneself about the complexities of social issues, listening to and amplifying marginalized voices, and actively working towards dismantling oppressive systems.

Authentic allyship is a crucial aspect of moving beyond performative activism. Allies must go beyond posting on social media or attending rallies to actively advocate for and support marginalized communities. This includes challenging one's own privilege, actively dismantling oppressive practices within one's spheres of influence, and centering the voices and experiences of marginalized individuals.

Moreover, authentic activism requires long-term commitment and sustained effort. Genuine change does not happen overnight, and it is essential to recognize that progress may be incremental. True activists remain dedicated to the cause, even in the face of setbacks and challenges.

Accountability is another critical element in moving beyond performative activism. Individuals and organizations must be willing to acknowledge and learn from their mistakes, accept feedback, and make necessary adjustments to their approach. This requires humility and a commitment to growth and improvement.

Moving beyond performative activism is essential in the pursuit of genuine awakening and social transformation. Authentic allyship, substance over appearance, sustained commitment, and accountability are key to effecting meaningful change. By actively engaging in substantive actions and amplifying marginalized voices, individuals can contribute to building a more just and equitable society.

### Building Inclusive Spaces for Awakening

It is crucial to create and foster inclusive spaces that encourage open dialogue, learning, and growth. Building such spaces allows individuals from diverse backgrounds to come together, share their experiences, and work collectively towards social transformation.

**Recognizing Diverse Perspectives:** Building inclusive spaces requires acknowledging and valuing the diversity of perspectives that individuals bring to the table. It is essential to create an environment where everyone feels heard and respected, regardless of their race, ethnicity, gender, sexuality, or any other characteristic.

**Cultivating Empathy and Compassion:** Empathy and compassion are foundational to creating inclusive spaces. Encouraging individuals to put themselves in others' shoes and understand their experiences fosters a deeper connection and a willingness to engage in genuine dialogue.

**Facilitating Difficult Conversations:** Inclusive spaces must be equipped to handle difficult conversations about privilege, power, and oppression. These conversations may be uncomfortable, but they are necessary for growth and understanding. Establishing ground rules for respectful communication can help navigate these discussions.

**Centering Marginalized Voices:** To build inclusive spaces, it is essential to center the voices and experiences of marginalized communities. Creating platforms for these voices to be heard and acknowledged is essential for genuine transformation.

**Continuous Learning and Unlearning:** Building inclusive spaces requires an ongoing commitment to learning and unlearning. It means challenging our own biases and assumptions and being open to new perspectives and knowledge.

**Addressing Power Dynamics:** Inclusive spaces should be mindful of power dynamics that may exist within the group. It is crucial to create a balanced environment where everyone's contributions are valued and no one dominates the conversation.

**Cultivating Allyship:** Building inclusive spaces involves fostering allyship and support among participants. Allies can use their privilege to uplift marginalized voices and actively work towards dismantling oppressive systems.

**Empowering Individuals:** Inclusive spaces should empower individuals to take action and make a difference in their communities. Participants should feel inspired and supported to engage in meaningful activism.

Building inclusive spaces for awakening is an essential aspect of the journey towards genuine transformation. By creating environments that value diverse perspectives, foster empathy, and center marginalized voices, individuals can work together to challenge oppressive systems and create a more just and equitable society. These spaces become the foundation for collective action and sustainable social change.

### The Intersectionality of Awakening

As individuals embark on the journey towards genuine awakening, it becomes evident that this process is deeply intertwined with the concept of intersectionality. Intersectionality recognizes that people's identities are shaped by the intersection of multiple social categories, such as race, gender, class, sexuality, and ability, and that these intersections influence their experiences and perspectives.

**Acknowledging Interconnected Systems of Oppression:** The intersectionality of awakening calls for acknowledging the interconnectedness of various systems of oppression. It recognizes that addressing one form of oppression without considering its intersections may not lead to comprehensive social change.

**Understanding Privilege and Marginalization:** Intersectionality prompts individuals to recognize their own privilege and how it intersects with various forms of marginalization. It challenges individuals to consider how their experiences may differ from others due to these intersections.

**Challenging Binary Thinking:** Embracing intersectionality challenges binary thinking and encourages individuals to see the complexity of human experiences. It invites them to embrace nuance and avoid oversimplification of social issues.

**Centering Marginalized Voices:** The intersectionality of awakening necessitates centering the voices and experiences of marginalized communities. It acknowledges that some voices have historically been silenced or ignored and seeks to rectify this imbalance.

**Empathy and Solidarity:** Intersectionality fosters empathy and solidarity among individuals from different backgrounds. It encourages recognizing shared struggles and working collectively towards a more equitable society.

**Addressing Inclusivity in Movements:** Embracing intersectionality is crucial for building inclusive social justice movements. It ensures that these movements are representative and relevant to the diverse communities they seek to serve.

**Embracing Complexity in Activism:** Activism informed by intersectionality is characterized by its complexity and adaptability. It acknowledges that social issues often have multifaceted causes and require nuanced solutions.

**Recognizing Agency and Empowerment:** The intersectionality of awakening acknowledges the agency of individuals to drive change in their communities. It empowers individuals to use their unique experiences and perspectives to advocate for social justice.

The intersectionality of awakening is a vital aspect of the journey towards genuine transformation. It calls for recognizing the complexity of human experiences and the interplay of various social identities and systems of oppression. Embracing intersectionality fosters inclusivity, empathy, and solidarity in social justice movements, making them more powerful and effective in challenging systemic inequalities. It is through this lens that individuals can forge a path towards a more equitable and compassionate world.

## Allyship and Collaborative Awakening

**Allyship as a Commitment:** Allyship is a crucial aspect of the journey towards genuine awakening. It involves individuals from privileged backgrounds committing to supporting marginalized communities by leveraging their privilege to challenge systemic inequalities.

**Listening and Learning:** True allyship requires active listening and a willingness to learn from marginalized voices. Allies must be receptive to feedback and continually educate themselves about the experiences of others.

**Using Privilege for Change:** Allyship involves using one's privilege to advocate for and uplift marginalized voices. Allies can leverage their access to resources, networks, and platforms to amplify marginalized narratives.

**Centering Marginalized Perspectives:** Collaborative awakening encourages centering marginalized perspectives in all discussions and decision-making processes. It recognizes that marginalized communities are experts on their own experiences and should lead in matters that affect them.

**Challenging Complicity:** Allies must confront and challenge their own complicity in perpetuating oppressive systems. This requires reflecting on internalized biases and actively working to dismantle them.

**Supporting Marginalized Leadership:** Collaborative awakening fosters a culture of supporting and empowering marginalized leadership. Allies should uplift and amplify the voices of those most impacted by injustice.

**Recognizing Interconnected Struggles:** Collaborative awakening highlights the interconnectedness of struggles and the need for solidarity between different marginalized communities. It rejects the idea of competition for limited resources and instead advocates for collective liberation.

**Acknowledging Mistakes and Growth:** Allies are not immune to making mistakes, but true allyship involves taking responsibility for those mistakes, apologizing when necessary, and committing to ongoing growth and improvement.

**Engaging in Intersectional Advocacy:** Collaborative awakening calls for intersectional advocacy that considers the overlapping identities and experiences of individuals. It recognizes that social justice issues are interconnected and require holistic approaches.

**Transformational Change:** Allyship and collaborative awakening lead to transformational change at both individual and systemic levels. It challenges power structures and paves the way for a more just and inclusive society.

Allyship and collaborative awakening are indispensable components of the journey towards genuine awakening. Through allyship, individuals leverage their privilege to uplift marginalized communities and challenge oppressive systems. Collaborative awakening fosters a culture of inclusivity, solidarity, and continuous learning. It empowers marginalized voices and recognizes the interconnectedness of social justice struggles. Together, allyship and collaborative awakening contribute to the creation of a more equitable and compassionate world for all.

The quest for genuine awakening is a complex and transformative journey that demands self-reflection, critical thinking, and active engagement with the world around us. Throughout this exploration, we have delved into the rise of corporate co-optation, the weaponization of "wokeness," the dangers of empty signifiers, and the importance of reclaiming narratives. We have also examined the role of structural racism, the power of authentic leadership, and the significance of allyship in fostering collective awakening.

Genuine awakening requires acknowledging the intricacies of power, privilege, and oppression that permeate society. It necessitates an understanding that liberation is not a singular destination but an ongoing process of unlearning and relearning. It involves recognizing that personal growth and social change are inherently interconnected.

The journey towards genuine awakening can be challenging and uncomfortable, as it requires confronting uncomfortable truths and recognizing our own complicity in oppressive systems. However, it is also a journey filled with hope, compassion, and solidarity. It calls us to foster inclusive spaces that value diverse perspectives and experiences. It demands that we amplify marginalized voices, center their narratives, and support their leadership.

Moreover, genuine awakening encourages us to engage in intersectional advocacy that seeks justice for all, regardless of identity or background. It empowers us to challenge the misappropriation of social justice language and to strive for clarity and authenticity in our communication.

Continue to remember that this is not a solo endeavor. Instead, it is a collective effort that requires collaboration, allyship, and the recognition that we are all interconnected. Together, we can create a world where compassion, equity, and justice prevail. Let us move forward

*"The shadow has been cast by subtle hues of deception; now is the time to break free from the chains of conformity"*

## CHAPTER 12
# REFLECTION AND RESPONSIBILITY

Now, collectively, we must embark on a journey of introspection and collective responsibility. We have explored the intricacies of "wokeness," corporate co-optation, the weaponization of language, structural racism, and the power of authentic storytelling. Now, we turn our gaze inward to reflect on the lessons learned and the actions required to create a more just and equitable world.

Reflection is a vital aspect of growth and transformation. As we navigate the complexities of social justice movements and the quest for genuine awakening, we must pause to examine our own biases, assumptions, and blind spots. It is through this introspection that we can identify our complicity in oppressive systems and make intentional choices to challenge and dismantle them.

However, reflection alone is not enough. Responsibility accompanies awareness. We bear a collective responsibility to engage in constructive dialogue, create inclusive spaces, and amplify marginalized voices. We must actively challenge the status quo, unlearn harmful narratives, and cultivate a culture of accountability and allyship.

Moreover, we must recognize that the journey towards social justice is ongoing and that progress is not linear. It demands resilience, empathy, and a commitment to continuous learning. It calls for solidarity and collaboration across diverse communities, acknowledging that liberation is interconnected and cannot be achieved in isolation.

Throughout this book, we have explored the complexities of navigating "wokeness" and the misappropriation of social justice language. Now, we are presented with an opportunity to reflect on our roles as individuals and as part of broader movements for change. As we engage in this process of self-reflection and collective responsibility, we must remain open to discomfort and challenge, for it is through this discomfort that true growth and transformation can occur.

Let us embark on this final chapter with a sense of purpose and commitment to fostering a more equitable and just world for all.

## The Power of Introspection

Introspection is a profound and transformative practice that enables individuals to explore their inner selves, thoughts, and emotions. It is a journey of self-awareness that helps us uncover our biases, assumptions, and deeply ingrained beliefs. By delving into the depths of our consciousness, we become more attuned to the ways in which our upbringing, socialization, and privilege shape our perspectives.

Through introspection, we confront our complicity in perpetuating oppressive systems and recognize our responsibility to challenge them. It is an uncomfortable yet essential process that enables us to break free from the constraints of societal conditioning and fosters personal growth and transformation.

Introspection invites us to confront our own biases and confront the uncomfortable truths we may have avoided. It is an act of vulnerability, requiring us to confront our privilege and acknowledge the ways in which we have benefited from systems of oppression.

This deep reflection on the self is not meant to induce guilt or shame but rather to inspire action and change. By acknowledging our biases and complicity, we become better equipped to dismantle oppressive structures and work towards justice and equity.

Introspection also plays a crucial role in fostering empathy and compassion. As we understand our own struggles and vulnerabilities, we become more attuned to the experiences of others. This empathy becomes the foundation for genuine allyship and collaborative awakening, where we stand alongside marginalized communities in their fight for justice.

Introspection acts as a compass, guiding us towards meaningful and authentic action. It is an ongoing process that requires patience, self-compassion, and a commitment to continuous growth.

As we engage in introspection, it is essential to create safe spaces for open dialogue and self-reflection. This can be achieved through practices like journaling, meditation, and participating in dialogue circles with like-minded individuals. It is through these intentional practices that we lay the groundwork for true reflection and assume the responsibility to dismantle oppressive systems, uplift marginalized voices, and contribute to a more equitable and just society.

## Acknowledging Mistakes and Imperfections

It is crucial to acknowledge that we are not infallible. As individuals committed to dismantling oppressive systems and promoting equity, it is natural that we may make mistakes along the way. However, what sets us apart is our willingness to acknowledge these mistakes and imperfections with humility and accountability.

Acknowledging mistakes requires us to confront our privilege and in-herent biases. It means recognizing when we have acted in ways that perpetuate harmful narratives or contribute to the marginalization of others. When we falter, owning up to our actions and understanding their impact is crucial to fostering trust within our communities.

Moreover, acknowledging mistakes and imperfections is a transformative act of vulnerability. It allows us to be authentic in our intentions and actions, demonstrating that we are committed to continuous learning and growth. Embracing imperfection as an inherent part of being human helps create spaces where others feel safe to do the same.

Through acknowledging our mistakes, we not only model accountability for others but also create opportunities for healing and reconciliation. It fosters a culture of compassion and understanding, where individuals can learn from one another's experiences and build stronger relationships.

However, acknowledging mistakes is not enough on its own. It must be accompanied by a genuine commitment to do better. This entails taking active steps to unlearn harmful behaviors, educate ourselves, and actively participate in dismantling oppressive structures.

As we embark on this journey, we must also be mindful not to center ourselves in conversations about oppression and social justice. Instead, we must amplify the voices of those directly impacted by systemic injustices and support their leadership in creating solutions.

Facing criticism, we must resist the urge to become defensive and instead approach it as an opportunity to learn and grow. By demonstrating humility and receptivity, we foster a culture of continuous improvement and create a collective environment that encourages others to engage in self-reflection and acknowledge their own mistakes.

Acknowledging mistakes and imperfections is a vital aspect of the path towards genuine awakening and effective activism. It involves embracing vulnerability, committing to growth, and amplifying marginalized voices. Through this process, we move closer to creating a more equitable and compassionate world for all.

## Cultivating Humility in Advocacy

Cultivating humility is a transformative and necessary virtue. It requires recognizing that we do not hold all the answers and that our perspectives may be limited by our own experiences and biases. Humility encourages us to listen, learn, and collaborate with others to foster more inclusive and effective advocacy.

One key aspect of cultivating humility is actively seeking out diverse voices and perspectives. Acknowledging that our own understanding of the world is not exhaustive, we must actively engage with individuals from different backgrounds and experiences. This involves being open to criticism and feedback, knowing that it offers valuable insights and opportunities for growth.

Humility also entails recognizing the complexities and nuances within social justice issues. While it is essential to address systemic oppression, we must avoid oversimplifying complex problems. Taking the time to understand the intricacies of various issues allows us to develop more thoughtful and impactful solutions.

Moreover, humility helps us navigate the potential pitfalls of performative activism. It encourages us to prioritize substance over optics and authenticity over virtue signaling. Rather than seeking recognition for our actions, we focus on the real impact of our advocacy efforts.

Additionally, cultivating humility allows us to engage in constructive dialogue with those who may not share our views. It enables us to approach discussions with an open mind and a willingness to learn from others, even when we disagree. This approach is more likely to bridge divides and foster understanding, rather than further polarizing conversations.

As advocates, we must recognize that we are part of a broader movement. Cultivating humility helps us avoid ego-driven activism and instead focus on collective progress. By centering the well-being of marginalized communities, we remain accountable to those we seek to support.

Humility is a crucial element of effective advocacy and genuine awakening. It encourages us to embrace diverse perspectives, navigate complexity, and prioritize authentic impact over empty gestures. Cultivating humility in advocacy allows us to foster more inclusive spaces and create lasting, positive change in our pursuit of social justice.

## Balancing Self-Care and Activism

Activists often find themselves fully immersed in the causes they champion. While passion and dedication are essential, it is equally crucial to strike a balance between activism and self-care. Balancing these two aspects is vital for sustaining long-term advocacy efforts and maintaining personal well-being.

Activism can be emotionally and mentally taxing, as it requires confronting deeply ingrained systems of oppression and working towards change. It is easy for activists to neglect their own well-being in the pursuit of justice for others. However, neglecting self-care can lead to burnout, exhaustion, and decreased effectiveness in advocacy work.

One key aspect of balancing self-care and activism is setting boundaries. It is crucial to establish limits on the time and emotional energy devoted to activism, ensuring that there is time for rest, relaxation, and self-reflection. By setting boundaries, activists can recharge and return to their advocacy efforts with renewed energy and focus.

Additionally, engaging in self-care practices is essential for maintaining resilience in the face of adversity. Self-care can take many forms, including spending time with loved ones, engaging in hobbies, and seeking support from a community of like-minded individuals. These practices can help combat feelings of isolation and overwhelm, providing a source of strength and support.

Moreover, recognizing the importance of self-care is not a sign of weakness but rather an acknowledgment of the humanity of activists.

It is essential to treat oneself with the same compassion and care that is extended to others.

Furthermore, activists should remember that self-care is not a luxury but a necessity for effective and sustainable advocacy. When activists prioritize their well-being, they can bring their whole selves to their work, ensuring that their efforts are more impactful and sustainable in the long run.

Balancing self-care and activism is crucial for both personal well-being and effective advocacy. By setting boundaries, engaging in self-care practices, and recognizing the importance of caring for oneself, activists can maintain resilience, avoid burnout, and continue to create positive change in the pursuit of social justice.

### Ethical Considerations in Advocacy

Advocacy for social justice requires a strong commitment to ethical principles and practices. As activists work towards creating positive change, they must navigate complex moral dilemmas and ensure that their actions align with their values and goals.

One critical ethical consideration in advocacy is the importance of transparency and honesty. Activists should be transparent about their objectives, funding sources, and any potential conflicts of interest. Transparency builds trust with the community and stakeholders, enhancing the credibility of the advocacy efforts.

Another ethical aspect of advocacy is respecting the autonomy and agency of the communities being served. Advocates must avoid imposing their solutions or agendas on communities without involving them in the decision-making process. A collaborative approach that empowers affected communities to have a voice in shaping the solutions is essential for ethical advocacy.

Furthermore, it is vital for activists to prioritize the well-being and safety of the individuals they are advocating for and with. This means considering the potential risks and consequences of their actions on vulnerable communities and taking steps to mitigate harm.

Integrity and consistency are also essential ethical considerations. Activists should remain true to their values and principles, even in the face of challenges or opposition. Being consistent in their advocacy efforts builds credibility and trust with supporters and the broader community.

Additionally, activists must be aware of the potential for unintended consequences of their actions. While advocacy aims to create positive change, there may be unintended negative consequences that arise. Ethical advocates actively assess the potential impacts of their actions and adjust their strategies to minimize harm.

Finally, ethical advocacy requires ongoing self-reflection and a willingness to learn and grow. It is essential for activists to be open to feedback and critique, acknowledge and learn from their mistakes, and continually improve their approach to advocacy.

Ethical considerations play a crucial role in effective and responsible advocacy. Transparency, respect for autonomy, prioritizing well-being, integrity, consideration of unintended consequences, and a commitment to continuous learning are all essential components of ethical advocacy in the pursuit of social justice.

## Amplifying Marginalized Voices

Amplifying marginalized voices is a critical responsibility for advocates working towards social justice. Too often, the voices of those who are most affected by systemic oppression and injustice are drowned out or ignored. By elevating these voices, activists can bring attention to the lived experiences and perspectives of marginalized communities and create a more inclusive and equitable movement.

One way to amplify marginalized voices is through inclusive representation. Advocacy efforts should strive to include diverse voices from different backgrounds, identities, and experiences. This means actively seeking out and elevating the voices of those who are often sidelined or underrepresented.

Listening and learning from marginalized communities is equally important. Genuine advocacy requires a deep understanding of the issues faced by marginalized groups, and that can only be achieved by listening to their stories, struggles, and aspirations. It is crucial to approach this listening with humility and empathy, acknowledging the power dynamics that may exist and centering the experiences of those who have been historically silenced.

Another way to amplify marginalized voices is by providing platforms and spaces for them to share their stories and perspectives. Advocates can collaborate with media, community organizations, and educational institutions to ensure that marginalized voices are heard and given the visibility they deserve.

Furthermore, allies have a vital role in amplifying marginalized voices. As advocates, they can use their privilege and influence to create spaces for others and to actively promote the visibility and recognition of marginalized communities.

Amplifying marginalized voices goes hand-in-hand with challenging dominant narratives. It involves disrupting the status quo and pushing back against systems of oppression that silence and erase the experiences of marginalized individuals.

Amplifying marginalized voices is a crucial responsibility for advocates committed to genuine social justice. By ensuring that the voices of those who have been historically marginalized are heard, valued, and respected, activists can build a more inclusive and equitable movement that centers the experiences of the most vulnerable and works towards meaningful and lasting change.

### Collaborative Activism and Allyship

Collaborative activism and allyship are essential components of effective social justice advocacy. While individual efforts are valuable, collective action and solidarity are powerful catalysts for change. Collaborative activism involves working together across diverse communities and identities to address systemic issues, recognizing that many forms of oppression are interconnected.

True allyship means supporting and standing in solidarity with marginalized communities without centering one's own experiences. It requires active listening, learning, and challenging one's own biases and privileges. Allies must take the time to understand the struggles faced by marginalized groups and use their platform to amplify their voices and advocate for their rights.

Collaborative activism and allyship also involve recognizing and respecting leadership from within marginalized communities. It is crucial to avoid tokenizing or co-opting their struggles and instead, follow their lead, needs, and priorities. Allies should work towards being accomplices, rather than saviors, in the fight for justice.

One way to foster collaborative activism is through coalition-building. Activists and advocacy organizations can come together to form alliances and work towards common goals, leveraging their collective strength and resources to effect meaningful change.

Furthermore, collaborative activism involves recognizing and addressing the intersections of identities and oppressions. It means acknowledging that individuals may experience multiple forms of discrimination and working to address these complexities in a holistic manner.

Importantly, collaboration and allyship require humility and a willingness to learn and grow. Allies must be open to feedback and critique from the communities they seek to support, and be willing to course-correct and adapt their approach as needed.

Collaborative activism and allyship are vital for building a strong, inclusive, and effective social justice movement. By coming together in solidarity, respecting and amplifying the voices of marginalized communities, and working collaboratively towards shared goals, activists can create meaningful and lasting change that benefits all.

## Holding Institutions and Systems Accountable

One of the crucial aspects of social justice advocacy is holding institutions and systems accountable for perpetuating inequality and oppression. Many of the problems faced by marginalized communities are deeply rooted in systemic issues that require institutional change.

Advocates must actively challenge and critique policies, practices, and structures that perpetuate discrimination and inequality. This may involve demanding transparency, accountability, and equity in decision-making processes within institutions. It may also mean advocating for policy changes that promote justice and fairness for all.

While holding institutions accountable, it is essential to consider the intersections of power and how they affect different groups. For example, addressing gender inequality may require acknowledging how it intersects with race, class, and other forms of oppression.

Transparency and public awareness play a vital role in holding institutions accountable. Advocates can utilize media, social platforms, and community engagement to shed light on injustices and demand change.

In this accountability, it is essential to address the systemic biases and discriminatory practices within them. This may involve implementing diversity and inclusion initiatives, unconscious bias training, and equitable hiring and promotion practices.

Community organizing and mobilization are powerful tools for holding institutions accountable. When individuals come together in protest or collective action, it sends a strong message to those in power that change is demanded.

Furthermore, intersectional advocacy can help address the ways that different systems of oppression interact and compound one another. By recognizing and addressing these intersections, advocates can work towards comprehensive and effective solutions.

Holding institutions and systems accountable is a fundamental part of social justice advocacy. It involves challenging systemic inequalities and demanding change at both the individual and institutional levels. By working collectively and strategically, activists can make a significant impact on dismantling oppressive structures and creating a more just and equitable society.

## Cultivating Empathy and Compassion

Empathy and compassion are essential qualities for effective social justice advocates. Cultivating these qualities allows advocates to connect with others, understand their struggles, and work towards genuine solutions that benefit all.

Empathy is the ability to put oneself in someone else's shoes, to understand and share their feelings, experiences, and perspectives. It involves actively listening to others and validating their emotions and experiences without judgment. Empathy allows advocates to build trust and rapport with individuals and communities they seek to support.

Compassion goes beyond understanding and extends to a genuine concern for the well-being of others. It drives advocates to take action and work towards alleviating the suffering of marginalized groups. Compassion is a driving force for transformative change, as it motivates advocates to push for justice and equity even when faced with challenges.

To cultivate empathy and compassion, advocates must actively engage in self-reflection and introspection. They must be willing to confront their biases, prejudices, and privileges and work towards being more inclusive and understanding.

Listening is a key skill in developing empathy and compassion. Advocates must actively listen to the stories and experiences of others, without interrupting or centering themselves in the conversation. This allows them to learn from diverse perspectives and understand the unique challenges faced by different communities.

Empathy and compassion are not just emotions; they require action. Advocates must use their empathy to inform their advocacy and decision-making processes. They should strive to create inclusive and safe spaces where marginalized voices can be heard and amplified.

In addition to empathy towards others, advocates must also practice self-compassion. Activism can be emotionally and mentally taxing, and advocates need to take care of themselves to avoid burnout and fatigue. Self-compassion allows advocates to acknowledge their own limitations and prioritize their well-being, ensuring they can continue the fight for justice in the long run.

Overall, cultivating empathy and compassion is crucial for effective and sustainable social justice advocacy. By embodying these qualities, advocates can build meaningful connections, create positive change, and contribute to building a more compassionate and equitable world.

### Navigating Criticism and Resistance

As social justice advocates, individuals often encounter criticism and resistance from various sources. Navigating these challenges is crucial for maintaining focus, resilience, and commitment to the cause.

Criticism can come from different directions, including those who disagree with the goals of the movement, opponents seeking to undermine the cause, or even fellow activists with differing perspectives. While some criticism may be constructive and provide opportunities for growth, others may be rooted in hostility or ignorance. Advocates must learn to discern between the two and be open to constructive feedback while also knowing when to stand firm in their convictions.

Resistance can take many forms, ranging from systemic barriers to personal attacks. The status quo may resist change, particularly when it threatens entrenched power structures. Advocates may face pushback from individuals or institutions that feel threatened by the demand for equity and justice.

To navigate criticism and resistance effectively, advocates must:

**Educate and Communicate:** Clearly articulating the goals and values of the movement can help dispel misconceptions and address criticism. Education is key to garnering support and building understanding.

**Self-Reflection:** Advocates should continuously reflect on their strategies and actions to ensure they are staying true to the cause and being accountable to the communities they represent.

**Building Coalitions:** Collaborating with like-minded individuals and groups can create a more significant impact and provide support in the face of resistance.

**Resilience:** Advocacy is often a long and challenging journey. Building emotional resilience and a strong support network is essential to weathering criticism and resistance.

**Responding Wisely:** While responding to criticism is important, advocates must choose their battles wisely. Engaging in endless debates with hostile individuals may not be productive.

**Maintain Focus:** Advocates should stay focused on the ultimate goals of the movement and not get derailed by distractions or minor setbacks.

**Acknowledge Limitations:** Advocates cannot single-handedly change the world. Understanding their limitations and collaborating with others can lead to more significant collective impact.

Navigating criticism and resistance is an ongoing challenge for social justice advocates. By remaining steadfast in their commitment, cultivating resilience, and embracing constructive feedback, advocates can continue to drive positive change and work towards a more just and equitable society.

Reflection and responsibility are paramount. This book has explored the complexities of "wokeness," the weaponization of social justice language, the structural roots of racism, the dangers of empty signifiers, and the power of reclaiming narratives. Throughout these chapters, the importance of authenticity, intersectionality, and empathy in activism has been emphasized.

Reflection allows advocates to critically assess their motivations, actions, and impact on the world around them. It helps build a deeper understanding of the root causes of social issues and the potential for change. Self-awareness and continuous learning enable advocates to navigate the challenges that arise and make informed decisions.

Responsibility involves recognizing the power and privilege that come with advocating for change and using that power responsibly. Advocates must be accountable to the communities they represent, ensuring that their work centers the voices of those most impacted by injustice.

Moreover, the responsibility lies not just with individuals but also with institutions and systems. Holding them accountable is crucial to dismantling systemic inequalities and achieving lasting change.

Genuine awakening and transformation require ongoing commitment. Advocacy is not a destination; it is a continuous journey of learning, growth, and unlearning. It demands courage to challenge the status quo, compassion to uplift marginalized voices, and resilience to weather the storms of resistance.

As we move forward in our advocacy, let us embrace humility, empathy, and inclusivity. Let us strive to be authentic allies, amplifying the voices of the oppressed and working collaboratively towards a more just and equitable world. Together, through reflection and responsibility, we can contribute to the collective efforts to dismantle oppression and build a society where everyone can thrive. The quest for social justice is a shared responsibility, and we all have a role to play.

*"Rewrite the scripts of enlightenment and replace illusion with authenticity."*

# SO WHERE DO WE GO FROM HERE?

Throughout this exploration of "wokeness," the weaponization of so-cial justice language, structural racism, empty signifiers, reclaiming narratives, and reflections on advocacy, one overarching theme has emerged: the transformative power of genuine awakening.

The journey began with an examination of the "Woke Industrial Complex," which highlighted the commodification and co-optation of social justice movements. The rise of empty signifiers, vague and ambiguous language, led to the dilution of meaningful discourse and the exploitation of genuine activism for profit and branding.

The misappropriation of "wokeness" by conservatives as a divisive tool further complicated the landscape. The dangerous distortion of social justice language obstructed productive dialogue and perpetuat-ed polarization, making it even more challenging to address the root causes of systemic inequalities.

To confront these issues, the importance of authentic activism became evident. Embracing personal narratives and intersectionality allowed for more inclusive and effective advocacy, amplifying marginalized voices and centering the experiences of those most impacted.

Collaborative activism and allyship were recognized as vital elements in this journey. By building inclusive spaces and recognizing complicity, advocates worked together to challenge the status quo and hold institutions accountable for their role in perpetuating injustice.

The power of storytelling and media representation became evident in reclaiming narratives and decentering dominant narratives. By elevating diverse perspectives, advocates sought to challenge harmful stereotypes and reframe the discourse on social justice.

To maintain the authenticity of their advocacy, individuals were encouraged to engage in introspection, unlearn harmful beliefs, and cultivate empathy. The recognition of imperfections and the willingness to learn from criticism allowed for growth and continuous improvement.

As the journey progressed, the dangers of empty signifiers and the manipulation of social justice language were underscored. These tactics obstructed genuine dialogue and hindered meaningful change. To combat this, advocates were urged to reimagine communication and language, ensuring that words aligned with meaningful actions.

The journey towards genuine awakening and responsible advocacy is not without its challenges. Navigating resistance and criticism requires resilience and unwavering commitment to social justice ideals. However, the power of collective consciousness and the recognition of the role of individuals in systems of oppression offer hope for transformative change.

This exploration of "wokeness" and social justice has revealed the complexity of the issues at hand. It has called for self-awareness, empathy, and humility in advocacy, reminding us that the journey towards a more just and equitable world is ongoing.

Through collaboration and the amplification of marginalized voices, we can challenge the misappropriation of social justice language and dismantle the systems that perpetuate inequality. By cultivating empathy and compassion, we can build inclusive spaces for genuine awakening and transformation.

As we move forward, let us carry the lessons learned on this journey, empowering ourselves and others to engage in reflective and responsible advocacy. Together, we can navigate the complexities of social justice and work towards a future that is truly inclusive, equitable, and just for all. The journey towards genuine awakening is one we must continue, armed with knowledge, empathy, and unwavering dedication to a better world.

### The Complexity of "Wokeness"

The exploration of "wokeness" and its various dimensions has revealed a multifaceted and complex landscape. "Wokeness" emerged as a powerful and necessary force in the fight for social justice, driven by a genuine desire to address systemic inequalities and uplift marginalized voices. However, its journey has not been without challenges and pitfalls.

The concept of "wokeness" is constantly evolving, making it difficult to pin down a precise definition. Its origins can be traced back to marginalized communities, where it represented an awakening to social injustices and a call for change. Over time, "wokeness" has been appropriated and misused, leading to the emergence of empty signifiers that dilute its impact and meaning.

The "Woke Industrial Complex" has commercialized and commodified social justice movements, turning activism into a marketable product. This capitalist co-optation has resulted in performative activism and the weaponization of "wokeness" against progressivism, further polarizing society.

Structural racism, implicit bias, and systemic inequities serve as the underlying root causes that "wokeness" seeks to address. The examination of criminal justice, education, housing, health, and economic disparities revealed how deeply embedded racism is in these systems, perpetuating inequality and injustice.

The complexity of "wokeness" is further heightened by the intersectionality of social justice issues. Recognizing the interconnectedness of various forms of oppression is crucial to understanding the broader picture of systemic inequities. Failing to acknowledge intersectionality can result in incomplete and insufficient solutions.

The danger of empty signifiers lies in their ability to co-opt and manipulate social justice language for nefarious purposes. Vague and ambiguous language can obscure genuine activism and hinder meaningful dialogue, ultimately undermining progress.

Reclaiming the narrative and elevating marginalized voices emerged as important strategies to counter the misappropriation of "wokeness" and dismantle dominant narratives. Authentic storytelling and media representation can challenge harmful stereotypes and bring attention to the experiences of marginalized communities.

Individuals must engage in introspection, unlearn harmful beliefs, and cultivate empathy. Recognizing mistakes and imperfections is essential in the journey of self-awareness, fostering humility in advocacy, and opening the door to growth and learning.

Throughout this exploration, the significance of allyship and collaborative activism was evident. Building inclusive spaces and amplifying marginalized voices are crucial in addressing systemic inequities and promoting collective empowerment.

The complexity of "wokeness" is mirrored in the complexity of the issues it seeks to address. Advancing social justice requires navigating a multitude of perspectives, histories, and experiences. It demands continuous reflection, responsibility, and resilience in the face of resistance and criticism.

As advocates for a more just and equitable world, we must recognize that the journey towards genuine awakening is ongoing. We must be aware of the challenges and ethical considerations that arise in the pursuit of social justice. Balancing self-care and activism is vital to ensuring our sustainability and effectiveness.

The complexity of "wokeness" lies in its ability to inspire and mobilize for change while simultaneously being vulnerable to appropriation and misrepresentation. The power of "wokeness" lies in its authenticity and commitment to justice, rooted in empathy and compassion. By navigating this complexity with humility and a genuine desire for collective empowerment, we can harness the true potential of "wokeness" as a force for positive social transformation.

## Unpacking the Misappropriation

The misappropriation of "wokeness" has been a complex and contentious phenomenon that has shaped public discourse on social justice and activism. As explored throughout this journey, the origins of "wokeness" can be traced back to marginalized communities seeking to address systemic inequalities and fight for justice. However, its co-optation and manipulation by various actors have led to its transformation into an empty signifier, devoid of its original meaning and intent.

The misappropriation of "wokeness" is often driven by political motives, with conservative forces using it as a pejorative to discredit and dismiss progressive ideals. The weaponization of "wokeness" against progressivism has created a divisive tool, amplifying polarization in society and hindering constructive dialogue.

This misappropriation has been further exacerbated by the media's role in disseminating and framing information. Information warfare and the manipulation of social justice language have clouded public understanding of "wokeness" and its genuine goals, perpetuating harmful stereotypes and contributing to societal division.

The landscape has created and environment where the quest for authenticity has become crucial. The power of authentic storytelling and reclaiming the narrative from marginalized voices is a response to combat the misappropriation of "wokeness." By elevating marginalized voices, the complexities and nuances of social justice issues are better understood, dismantling empty signifiers and challenging dominant narratives.

At the heart of this issue is the need for self-awareness and introspection. Recognizing mistakes and imperfections and cultivating humility in advocacy can lead to a more genuine awakening. Allies play a vital role in collaborative activism, standing alongside marginalized communities and amplifying their voices.

Building inclusive spaces and fostering collective consciousness are essential steps towards holding institutions and systems accountable for their complicity in perpetuating systemic inequities. Cultivating empathy and compassion is key to fostering a sense of interconnectedness that transcends the barriers of identity and privilege.

However, it is not without challenges. Navigating criticism and resistance is an inevitable part of the journey towards dismantling the misappropriation of "wokeness." It requires resilience and a commitment to self-reflection and learning, acknowledging that progress is not linear.

Unpacking the misappropriation of "wokeness" is a complex and ongoing process. It requires collective effort, a commitment to justice, and a dedication to authentic activism. By understanding the origins and evolution of "wokeness," recognizing its misappropriation, and engaging in genuine dialogue, we can navigate the complexities and harness the true potential of "wokeness" as a force for positive social change.

## The Quest for Authenticity

The quest for authenticity has emerged as a powerful response to the misappropriation of "wokeness" and the challenges faced by social justice movements. Throughout this journey, we have explored how the genuine pursuit of justice and equity has been co-opted and diluted, leading to the emergence of empty signifiers and divisive rhetoric. However, the reclaiming of authenticity has opened new avenues for progress and positive change.

At the heart of the quest for authenticity lies the power of personal narratives. By embracing personal experiences and amplifying marginalized voices, the complexities and nuances of social justice issues are brought to the forefront. Through authentic storytelling, the misappropriation of "wokeness" can be dismantled, and dominant narratives can be challenged, making way for a more inclusive and empathetic society.

Navigating allyship with authenticity is another critical aspect of this quest. True allies recognize their privilege and use it to uplift marginalized communities, rather than co-opting their struggles for personal gain. Collaborative activism and allyship foster collective awakening, emphasizing the power of solidarity and collective consciousness in driving meaningful change.

The role of media and information sharing cannot be understated in the quest for authenticity. Responsible media practices that prioritize accuracy and inclusivity can counteract the manipulation of social justice language and combat misinformation. Media outlets must be vigilant in amplifying genuine narratives and elevating the voices of those directly impacted by social injustices.

Furthermore, authenticity demands introspection and acknowledgment of mistakes and imperfections. Cultivating humility in advocacy is essential to foster a culture of learning and growth, moving beyond performative activism and towards genuine engagement with social justice causes.

Building inclusive spaces is pivotal in this journey. Creating environments that value diverse perspectives and empower marginalized communities to have a seat at the table can lead to more robust and comprehensive solutions to systemic issues.

Intersectionality emerges as a guiding framework in the quest for authenticity. Recognizing the interconnectedness of various forms of oppression allows for a more holistic understanding of social justice struggles. By embracing intersectionality, we can address the unique challenges faced by different communities and work towards a more equitable world.

Throughout this journey, we have learned that the pursuit of authenticity is not without challenges. Criticism and resistance are inevitable, but resilience and commitment to the cause can overcome these hurdles.

The quest for authenticity is a continuous and transformative process. By reclaiming the narrative, amplifying marginalized voices, and embracing collective consciousness, we can navigate the complexities of "wokeness" and social justice. It requires self-awareness, empathy, and a willingness to unlearn and relearn. Through genuine engagement and responsible advocacy, we can dismantle empty signifiers and confront the misappropriation of "wokeness," ultimately moving towards a more just and equitable society.

## Towards a Genuine Awakening

The journey towards a genuine awakening is a profound and transformative one, marked by self-awareness, unlearning, empathy, and collective consciousness. Throughout this exploration, we have encountered the complexities of "wokeness" and witnessed its misappropriation, but we have also discovered the power of reclaiming authenticity, building inclusive spaces, and amplifying marginalized voices. Now, as we approach the conclusion of this journey, we stand at the threshold of genuine awakening.

The quest for authenticity and the recognition of empty signifiers have highlighted the importance of introspection and humility. Acknowledging our mistakes and imperfections is not a sign of weakness but rather a testament to our commitment to growth and learning. As we engage in activism, it is crucial to balance self-care with advocacy, recognizing that our well-being is intimately connected with the well-being of others.

Ethical considerations must guide our actions, ensuring that we uphold the values of justice and equity while avoiding the pitfalls of performative activism. Collaborative activism and allyship become vehicles for collective awakening, transcending individual efforts and fostering solidarity across diverse communities.

At the heart of this journey lies the intersectionality of awakening. Understanding the interconnectedness of various forms of oppression allows us to address the root causes of systemic issues and forge a more comprehensive and inclusive path towards change. By amplifying marginalized voices and recognizing their lived experiences, we dismantle the walls of privilege that impede genuine progress.

Media representation and responsible information sharing are essential in this endeavor. The media's power to shape narratives and influence public opinion cannot be underestimated. It is incumbent upon us to hold media outlets accountable for accurate and inclusive reporting, ensuring that authentic stories are given the space they deserve.

Criticism and resistance may arise as we navigate this awakening, but the resilience and commitment to our values will sustain us. Embracing feedback and engaging in constructive dialogue can lead to growth and refinement, ultimately strengthening our collective impact.

The journey towards a genuine awakening is an ongoing and transformative process. It requires courage, humility, and a dedication to building inclusive spaces where all voices are heard and respected. By recognizing the complexity of "wokeness" and the misappropriation it has faced, we pave the way for authentic engagement with social justice issues. This awakening is not a destination but a continuous evolution towards a more just, equitable, and compassionate world.

As we conclude this exploration, let us carry the lessons learned and the principles of authenticity, empathy, and collaboration with us. May this genuine awakening be the catalyst for transformative change, inspiring us to engage with social justice issues in a way that is grounded in respect, empathy, and a commitment to dismantling systems of oppression. Together, we can build a brighter and more equitable future for all.

## Reflection and Responsibility

We have discussed the complexities of "wokeness," unearthing its misappropriation, and seeking a path towards genuine awakening. We have explored the power of introspection, acknowledging mistakes, and cultivating humility as key pillars of authentic advocacy. Balancing self-care and activism has taught us the importance of nurturing our well-being while engaging in the fight for justice.

Ethical considerations have guided us in navigating the challenges of advocacy, ensuring that our actions align with our values and promote the greater good. Collaborative activism and allyship have demonstrated the strength that lies in unity, fostering collective consciousness to dismantle systems of oppression.

Amplifying marginalized voices has been at the core of this journey, recognizing the vital importance of including diverse perspectives to create a more inclusive world. Through responsible media representation and information sharing, we can challenge narratives that perpetuate stereotypes and advocate for a more accurate portrayal of marginalized communities.

As we move forward, we must navigate criticism and resistance with resilience, learning from feedback to improve our strategies and remain steadfast in our commitment to change. Embracing empathy and compassion enables us to connect with others' experiences, fostering a deeper understanding of the issues we fight for.

Throughout this reflection, the responsibility of individuals and institutions in upholding justice has become evident. We must hold ourselves accountable for our actions and actively seek to dismantle oppressive systems, while also holding institutions accountable for perpetuating inequality.

Ultimately, this journey of reflection and responsibility is a call to action. It is a call to be conscious of our own privileges and biases, and to continuously challenge ourselves to grow and unlearn harmful beliefs. It is a call to be aware of the power dynamics at play and to actively work towards creating more equitable and inclusive spaces.

We must take responsibility not only for our individual actions but also for our role in society at large. By acknowledging our complicity in systems of oppression, we can begin to dismantle them from within and create a more just and equitable world.

The journey of reflection and responsibility is a never-ending one. It requires constant self-awareness, humility, and a commitment to learning and growing. It demands that we listen to the experiences of others, amplify marginalized voices, and challenge the status quo.

By taking responsibility for our actions and advocating for justice, we contribute to the collective efforts towards genuine awakening. Each of us has a role to play in this journey, and together, we can create a more compassionate, inclusive, and equitable world for everyone. Let us embrace this responsibility with open hearts and minds, as we continue to work towards a brighter and more just future.

### The Path Forward

The journey we have undertaken in exploring the complexities of "wokeness," unpacking its misappropriation, seeking authenticity, and embracing genuine awakening has been both enlightening and challenging. As we conclude this exploration, we must now look to the path forward, understanding that this work is ongoing and requires continued dedication and commitment.

**One.** We must recognize the importance of ongoing education and learning. The issues of social justice, systemic racism, and inequality are deeply ingrained in our society, and dismantling these structures requires a deep understanding of their historical context and their present manifestations. We must continually educate ourselves and others, engage in critical conversations, and seek out diverse perspectives to expand our knowledge and challenge our assumptions.

**Two.** We must actively engage in allyship and collaborative activism. The struggle for justice and equality is not the responsibility of the marginalized alone; it is the responsibility of everyone. As allies, we must listen, amplify marginalized voices, and follow their leadership while being mindful not to co-opt or overshadow their experiences.

**Three.** We must hold ourselves and others accountable. This includes holding institutions and systems accountable for perpetuating injustice and ensuring that we are personally living up to our values and commitments. We must be willing to acknowledge our mistakes, learn from them, and do better.

**Four.** We must cultivate empathy and compassion. Social justice work can be emotionally taxing, and it is essential to take care of ourselves and others throughout the journey. By embracing empathy and compassion, we can create a supportive community that uplifts and sustains us in the fight for justice.

**Five.** We must engage in meaningful and inclusive activism. This means recognizing that different communities have different needs and challenges and tailoring our advocacy efforts accordingly. It means working collaboratively across lines of difference and building coalitions that amplify collective voices.

**Six.** We must reclaim the narrative and challenge the misappropriation of "wokeness." By using language responsibly, authentically, and in solidarity with those fighting for justice, we can create a counter-narrative that reflects the true values of the movement.

The path forward is not linear, and there will undoubtedly be obstacles and setbacks along the way. However, by centering our actions in empathy, compassion, and inclusivity, we can move closer to a more equitable and just society.

The journey towards social justice is complex and multifaceted. It requires ongoing reflection, responsibility, and a commitment to growth and learning. It calls for individual and collective action, and it demands that we continually challenge and dismantle the systems of oppression that perpetuate inequality.

As we move forward, let us remember that the struggle for justice is not an isolated endeavor but a collective movement. Together, we can create a more equitable, compassionate, and inclusive world where everyone's rights and dignity are respected. The path forward is a journey of hope, courage, and solidarity, and it is one that we must all embark on to create a better future for generations to come.

## A Call to Action

As we conclude our exploration of "wokeness" and social justice, we are left with a profound call to action. The issues we have discussed are not abstract concepts; they have real and tangible effects on the lives of countless individuals and communities. We cannot afford to be passive bystanders; we must take action to create the change we want to see in the world.

The first step in our call to action is to recognize our own privilege and biases. It is essential to confront and unlearn the unconscious prejudices we may hold and actively work towards becoming more inclusive and equitable individuals. This introspection and self-awareness will lay the foundation for our journey towards becoming allies in the fight for justice.

Next, we must engage in ongoing education and learning. It is not enough to be aware of social justice issues; we must continually seek to expand our knowledge and understanding. By listening to and learning from the experiences of marginalized communities, we can become more informed advocates for change.

We must also be willing to use our voices and platforms to amplify marginalized voices and stories. Whether it be through social media, art, writing, or public speaking, we can play a crucial role in elevating the narratives of those who have been historically silenced. By centering these voices, we can challenge the misappropriation of "wokeness" and create a more authentic and inclusive movement.

Collaborative activism is another critical aspect of our call to action. By working together across communities and identities, we can build a more powerful and effective movement for change. We must bridge the gaps that have historically divided us and form strong alliances based on shared values and goals.

In addition to external action, we must also prioritize self-care and well-being. The work of social justice can be emotionally and mentally taxing, and it is essential to take care of ourselves and each other. This means setting boundaries, seeking support, and creating spaces for healing and reflection.

Lastly, we must advocate for systemic change and hold institutions accountable. Whether it be in our workplaces, schools, or governments, we must challenge policies and practices that perpetuate inequality and discrimination. By demanding accountability and transparency, we can push for meaningful and lasting change.

The call to action is not a one-time event; it is an ongoing commitment to justice and equality. It requires us to stay engaged, even in the face of adversity and resistance. It calls for courage, persistence, and solidarity with those who are most affected by systemic injustice.

The journey towards social justice is a collective effort that demands action from all of us. It requires us to challenge our own beliefs and biases, to listen and learn from marginalized voices, and to be vocal advocates for change. By embracing this call to action, we can work towards a more equitable, inclusive, and compassionate society where everyone can thrive. Let us stand together in this endeavor, united by our shared commitment to justice and humanity.

## Acknowledging Ongoing Challenges

As we reflect on our journey through the complexities of "wokeness" and social justice, it is essential to acknowledge the ongoing challenges we face in the pursuit of a more just and equitable world. While our efforts are vital, we must recognize that the road ahead is not without obstacles and setbacks.

One of the first challenges we encounter is the deeply ingrained nature of systemic racism, sexism, homophobia, and other forms of oppression. These structures have been woven into the fabric of society for centuries, and dismantling them requires persistent and collective action. The work of social justice is not a quick fix; it is a generational struggle that demands resilience and perseverance.

Additionally, the misappropriation of "wokeness" by various actors, including political opportunists and corporations, poses a significant challenge to the authenticity of social justice movements. Empty signifiers and performative activism can dilute the impact of genuine advocacy, creating confusion and divisiveness. Navigating this terrain requires us to remain vigilant and critical in our assessments of motives and intentions.

Furthermore, the polarized nature of contemporary discourse presents another obstacle. The echo chambers of social media and the prevalence of misinformation can lead to the entrenchment of opposing views, making it difficult to find common ground and engage in constructive dialogue. Overcoming this challenge necessitates seeking out spaces that foster empathy, understanding, and respectful debate.

We must also confront the structural barriers that hinder the voices of marginalized communities from being heard and acknowledged. Systemic inequalities in education, employment, healthcare, and housing perpetuate the marginalization of certain groups, making it imperative for us to address these disparities as part of our broader social justice efforts.

While progress has been made in various areas, it is crucial to avoid complacency and recognize that the struggle for social justice is ongoing. The fight against oppression and discrimination cannot be won with one-time gestures or token efforts. It requires a sustained commitment to transformative change at both individual and systemic levels.

Lastly, as we move forward, we must guard against burnout and ex-haustion. Engaging in activism can be emotionally draining, and self-care is essential for sustaining our efforts. Cultivating a sense of community and support can help us navigate the challenges that lie ahead.

Acknowledging the ongoing challenges in our pursuit of social justice is critical for maintaining focus and determination. The complexity of "wokeness" requires us to navigate a landscape fraught with misap-propriation, polarization, and systemic barriers. However, by staying true to the principles of authenticity, intersectionality, and allyship, we can make meaningful progress towards a more just and equitable world. It is a journey that requires collective action, empathy, and continuous learning. Let us embrace the challenges with courage and solidarity, knowing that every step forward brings us closer to a future where all individuals are seen, heard, and valued.

## A Vision for a More Just Future

As we reflect on the complexities of "wokeness," social justice, and the challenges that lie ahead, we must hold on to a vision of a more just and equitable future. This vision is not an abstract ideal; it is a tangible and achievable goal that requires our collective efforts and unwavering commitment.

In this envisioned future, systemic racism, sexism, and all forms of oppression have been dismantled. Institutions and systems have been reimagined to be inclusive, fair, and accessible to all. Marginalized voices are not only heard but actively sought out and amplified, ensur-ing that decision-making processes are representative and reflective of the diverse communities they serve.

In this future, empathy and compassion are at the heart of our inter-actions. We have learned to listen deeply, engage in genuine dialogue, and hold space for the lived experiences of others. We recognize that genuine allyship is not just about showing support but actively advocating for the rights and dignity of others.

Education has become a powerful tool for transformation, challenging the status quo and promoting critical thinking. It is a space where diverse perspectives and histories are acknowledged and celebrated, and where the curriculum is inclusive of all cultures, identities, and contributions to society.

Economic inequities have been addressed through policies that prioritize the welfare of the most vulnerable members of society. Wealth and resources are distributed more equitably, providing everyone with the opportunity to thrive and prosper.

In this future, the environment is protected, and the impact of climate change is mitigated. We have recognized the intersectionality between social and environmental justice, understanding that the most vulnerable communities are disproportionately affected by environmental degradation.

Political systems are transparent, accountable, and responsive to the needs and aspirations of the people. Civic engagement is encouraged and facilitated, empowering individuals to participate actively in shaping their communities and societies.

Media and information sharing have become responsible and ethical, committed to accurate representation and combatting misinformation. Authentic storytelling and narratives that uplift and empower have replaced empty signifiers and performative gestures.

This vision is not a distant dream; it is within our reach. Achieving this future requires us to stay committed to self-awareness, empathy, and genuine dialogue. It calls for us to challenge ourselves and others to unlearn biases, confront privilege, and take responsibility for our actions.

As we navigate the complexities of "wokeness" and social justice, let us hold onto this vision as a guiding light. Let it motivate and inspire us to keep pushing forward, even in the face of challenges and setbacks.

The journey towards a more just future is ongoing, and each step we take brings us closer to realizing the world we aspire to create.

Together, let us embrace the call to action, build authentic alliances, and foster empathy and compassion. By working collaboratively and with resilience, we can bring about the transformative change needed to build a world where justice, equity, and dignity are afforded to all.

## Empowering Readers

As this was a comprehensive exploration of "wokeness," its evolution, misappropriation, and the quest for authenticity, we have provided an insightful argument that speaks to the complexities of social justice movements and the challenges they face. We have recognized the power and potential of genuine awakening and the importance of reflection and responsibility in advocacy. As we conclude this journey, our focus shifts to empowering readers to become catalysts for positive change in their communities and beyond.

Education is the foundation of empowerment. By equipping ourselves with knowledge about the historical context of social injustices, the impact of systemic inequities, and the nuances of identity, we become better equipped to navigate the complexities of "wokeness" and social justice. By seeking diverse perspectives and engaging with credible sources, we can foster critical thinking and discernment, enabling us to recognize empty signifiers and manipulations of language.

Reclaiming the narrative will be difficult. It will be essential for readers to become active participants in shaping and amplifying authentic stories. By elevating marginalized voices and supporting their efforts to be heard, we can challenge dominant narratives and promote inclusivity. Readers can play a vital role in media representation, advocating for responsible journalism that accurately reflects the diverse experiences and struggles of different communities.

Beyond knowledge and awareness, empathy and compassion are the cornerstones of effective activism. Readers can cultivate empathy by actively listening to the lived experiences of others and striving

SO WHERE DO WE GO FROM HERE? | 257

to understand their perspectives. Empathy creates a bridge between different communities, allowing for collaborative activism and the forging of meaningful alliances.

Moreover, empowering readers means recognizing the significance of their actions and choices. By acknowledging their complicity in systems of oppression and working towards unlearning biases, readers can become advocates for change. Each small act, each conversation, and each moment of self-reflection can contribute to the collective journey towards a more just and equitable world.

It is crucial for readers to navigate criticism and resistance with resilience and humility. Challenging the status quo and advocating for social justice often invites pushback, but staying true to one's values and commitments is essential. Embracing constructive feedback and learning from mistakes are vital aspects of growth and progress. To challenge the misappropriation of "wokeness" and social justice language, we must be steadfast in our commitment to authenticity, empathy, and genuine advocacy.

The path forward is illuminated by the collective effort of individuals who dare to question, listen, and act. As readers take on the responsibility of being advocates for change, we must remember that we are not alone on this journey. Together, we can build a more just and equitable world, one conversation, one action, and one step at a time. Empowered readers have the potential to create lasting impact, and in doing so, they contribute to the transformative evolution of society.

## Final Thoughts

This has been a very exhaustive journey. And it still continues. We have explored the weaponization and misappropriation of "wokeness," the quest for authenticity, the call for genuine awakening, and the importance of reflection and responsibility. As we reach the end of this exploration, it is essential to reflect on the profound impact this knowledge can have on our lives and the world we inhabit.

Our final thoughts are a reminder that this journey does not end here. The exploration of "wokeness" and social justice is an ongoing process, requiring continuous learning, unlearning, and relearning. As we engage in this process, we must remain open to new ideas, perspectives, and experiences. Each person's unique journey informs and enriches the collective understanding of social justice, driving us closer to a more equitable world.

We must remember that meaningful change often encounters opposition. However, this resistance can be seen as a testament to the significance of the work we undertake. By acknowledging criticism and learning from it, we strengthen the foundations of our advocacy and push forward with greater conviction.

As we reclaim the narrative and elevate marginalized voices, we begin to see the power of stories to foster empathy, compassion, and connection. Stories can bridge the gaps between communities, reminding us of our shared humanity and common struggles. By amplifying these voices, we empower those who have long been silenced and pave the way for a more inclusive society.

The road to a more just future is not without obstacles, and it requires collective action and allyship. By collaborating with others, we combine our strengths and resources, multiplying the impact of our efforts. Together, we can build bridges between different communities and advocate for social justice with a unified voice.

Through empowerment, self-awareness, and empathy, we also recognize the vital role of education. Education is the catalyst that sparks change, enabling us to challenge dominant narratives, address systemic injustices, and take action for social progress.

Our call to action is an invitation to readers to be active participants in the pursuit of justice. Through our choices, our conversations, and our advocacy, we can make a difference. We encourage readers to engage in their communities, initiate meaningful dialogues, and seek opportunities to promote equality.

Finally, we express gratitude to all those who have taken this journey with us, embracing the complexities of "wokeness" and social justice. By working together, we have laid the groundwork for a more inclusive and equitable world. As we continue our exploration, we hold on to the hope that our efforts will create a brighter, more just future for generations to come. The power lies within each of us to create meaningful change, and it is with this belief that we set forth on the path towards a more compassionate and empathetic society. Let us walk this path together, uplifting one another, and recognizing the potential for transformation that exists within us all.

### Farewell

As we bid farewell to this journey of understanding "wokeness" and social justice, we carry with us the knowledge and insights gained from exploring the complexities of this ever-evolving landscape. Our minds have been expanded, our perspectives broadened, and our hearts stirred with a renewed commitment to creating a more just and equitable world.

We extend our gratitude to all those who have joined us on this exploration - the thinkers, the activists, the scholars, and the dreamers. Each of you has played a significant role in shaping the discourse and challenging the status quo. Your dedication to social justice and your tireless pursuit of equality inspire us to continue this important work.

As we part ways, we encourage each reader to take the lessons learned from this journey and apply them in their lives and communities. Engage in meaningful conversations with empathy and humility, recognizing that everyone's experiences and struggles are unique. Embrace the complexities of "wokeness" and social justice, recognizing that progress often comes in small steps and that setbacks are opportunities for growth.

While our exploration may have reached its conclusion, our commitment to social justice and the pursuit of a more equitable world continues. Let us not forget that the fight for justice extends beyond the pages of this text. It manifests in our daily actions, in our interactions with others, and in the choices we make. Every moment presents an opportunity to create change, and every act of kindness and understanding contributes to the collective effort.

We urge readers to remain vigilant against the misappropriation and distortion of "wokeness" and social justice language. It is easy for these concepts to become empty signifiers, devoid of their transformative power, but we must not allow that to happen. Stay informed, question prevailing narratives, and strive for nuance and depth in our understanding of social justice issues.

As we bid farewell, we also recognize that the journey of understanding "wokeness" and social justice is ongoing. The world is constantly changing, and so too must our advocacy and activism. We must be adaptable and receptive to new ideas, always seeking to improve and refine our approach to social justice.

We thank each reader for joining us on this exploration. It is our hope that this text has been both enlightening and empowering, inspiring you to take action and become agents of positive change. Farewell for now, but let us carry the spirit of this journey with us always, as we continue to work towards a more just, equitable, and compassionate world for all.

*"Rewrite the scripts of enlightenment and replace illusion with authenticity."*

# ACKNOWLEDGMENTS

This endeavor, Straight Jackin', stands as a testament to the collective effort, dedication, and support from an array of individuals who have contributed to its fruition. As I reflect on this journey, I am humbled by the immense love and encouragement that has surrounded me. The profound sense of gratitude that swells within me is a testament to the power of community and collaboration.

First and foremost, I extend my deepest appreciation to the many scholars, activists, and thinkers whose works have shaped my understanding and informed the ideas presented in this book. Their tireless pursuit of knowledge and their commitment to social justice have been a guiding light throughout this intellectual expedition.

To my incredible team of editors, thank you for your unwavering belief in the importance of this project and for your meticulous attention to detail. Your invaluable insights and constructive feedback have undoubtedly enriched the final product.

I am indebted to the numerous individuals who generously shared their personal experiences and stories, providing a kaleidoscope of perspectives that have illuminated the complexities of our cultural vernacular. Your courage and openness have made this book a more profound and impactful exploration.

A special note of gratitude goes to the Montague Collection, Clinton Byrd, Margaret Byrd Jones (my mom, his sister), my mentors, and academic advisors over time, whose wisdom and guidance have shaped my scholarship and nurtured my passion for social justice. Your unwavering support and belief in my potential have been pivotal in my growth as a thinker and an advocate.

To my friends and family, you have been my rock and my refuge throughout this journey. Your love, encouragement, and understanding have sustained me during moments of doubt and difficulty. Your unwavering support has given me the strength to persevere and to believe in the transformative power of this work.

I must also acknowledge the countless activists and advocates who tirelessly fight for justice and equality in our communities. Your courage and resilience have inspired me to continue this pursuit of knowledge and to strive for change in the face of adversity.

The publishing team, with their dedication and expertise, has played a pivotal role in bringing this vision to life. Thank you for your tireless efforts and for believing in the importance of amplifying marginalized voices.

Lastly, I express my deepest gratitude to the readers of Straight Jackin'. Your engagement with this work is an affirmation of its relevance and significance. It is my hope that this book sparks conversations, inspires critical thinking, and fosters a deeper understanding of the issues at hand.

I stand before you, deeply moved by the unwavering support that has propelled Straight Jackin' forward. To each and every person who has contributed to this project in big and small ways, I extend my heartfelt gratitude. Together, we navigate the complexities of our cultural vernacular, striving for a more just and compassionate world. It is with deep appreciation and a profound sense of responsibility that I offer my heartfelt acknowledgments.

# BIBLIOGRAPHY

Rose, T. (1994). "Black Noise: Rap Music and Black Culture in Contemporary America." Wesleyan University Press.

Coates, T. N. (2015). "Between the World and Me." Spiegel & Grau.

DiAngelo, R. (2018). "White Fragility: Why It's So Hard for White People to Talk About Racism." Beacon Press.

Dyson, M. E. (2017). "Tears We Cannot Stop: A Sermon to White America." St. Martin's Press.

Kendi, I. X. (2019). "How to Be an Antiracist." One World.

Lorde, A. (2017). "Your Silence Will Not Protect You: Essays and Poems." Silver Press.

Mensa, V. (2019). "Straight from the Source: 'Woke' Isn't Just a Buzzword—It's a Whole Mindset." GQ.

Oluo, I. (2018). "So You Want to Talk About Race." Seal Press.

Rankine, C. (2014). "Citizen: An American Lyric." Graywolf Press.

Solórzano, D. G., & Bernal, D. D. (2001). "Examining Transformational Resistance Through a Critical Race and LatCrit Theory Framework: Chicana and Chicano Students in an Urban Context." Urban Education, 36(3), 308-342.

Steele, C. M. (1990). "Race and the Schooling of Black Americans." The Atlantic Monthly, 265(5), 68-78.

Tuck, E., & Yang, K. W. (2012). "Decolonization is Not a Metaphor." Decolonization: Indigeneity, Education & Society, 1(1).

Yosso, T. J. (2005). "Whose culture has capital? A critical race theory discussion of community cultural wealth." Race Ethnicity and Education, 8(1), 69-91.

Zinn, H. (2009). "A People's History of the United States." HarperCollins.

hooks, b. (2014). "Feminism Is for Everybody: Passionate Politics." Routledge.

Ahmed, S. (2012). "On Being Included: Racism and Diversity in Institutional Life." Duke University Press.

Delgado, R., & Stefancic, J. (2017). "Critical Race Theory: An Introduction." NYU Press.

Crenshaw, K. (1989). "Demarginalizing the Intersection of Race and Sex: A Black Feminist Critique of Antidiscrimination Doctrine, Feminist Theory and Antiracist Politics." University of Chicago Legal Forum, 1989(1), 139-167.

Collins, P. H. (2015). "Intersectionality's Definitional Dilemmas." Annual Review of Sociology, 41, 1-20.

Davis, A. Y. (2016). "Freedom Is a Constant Struggle: Ferguson, Palestine, and the Foundations of a Movement." Haymarket Books.

hooks, b. (1994). "Teaching to Transgress: Education as the Practice of Freedom." Routledge.

King, M. L. Jr. (1963). "Letter from Birmingham Jail." In "Why We Can't Wait." Beacon Press.

West, C. (1993). "Race Matters." Vintage.

# INDEX